WHILE
AMERICA
PLAYED

WHILE AMERICA PLAYED

CECIL TODD

New Leaf Press

P.O. BOX 311, GREEN FOREST, AR 72638

FIRST EDITION
1984

Typesetting by SPACE
(Sharp Printing & Computer Enterprises)
Berryville, AR 72616

Library of Congress Catalog Card Number: 84-061914
International Standard Book Number: 0-89221-116-4

Printed in the United States of America

DEDICATION

This book is warmly and affectionately dedicated to the memory of Mervin J. Stillwell. He was promoted to glory on July 23, 1976 and to his loving and caring helpmate, Marguerite.

These two choice servants of our Lord, have always encouraged me to keep going for God!

TABLE OF CONTENTS

PREFACE

This explosive book is dedicated to stopping the deep erosion of America's religious freedoms.

Satanic forces, "Hatched in Hell" have been unleashed on our nation during the past several years, and since America was busy "playing" instead of "praying," many precious freedoms have been stolen!

In 1925, they stole the teaching of Biblical creation from our public schools and replaced it with the Theory of Evolution!

In 1948, religious instruction was stopped in most public schools!

In 1962, prayer and Bible reading was stolen from our school kids . . . in 1973, they said it was all right to kill the little babies before they were born . . . in 1978, the singing of Christmas Carols was stopped in many schools . . . in 1980, they stripped the Ten Commandments from the walls of our school classrooms . . . in 1981, they started removing crosses from the city parks . . . in 1982, they padlocked a House of Worship in Louisville, Nebraska and put the preacher in jail!

In 1983, many school kids were stopped from carrying their own Bibles to school and were forbidden from saying "Grace" for their meals! In 1984, public school teachers started dropping the words, "Under God" from the Pledge of Allegiance" and in other schools the American flag was removed from the classrooms!

America must stop her playing and start praying . . . stop her feasting and start fasting! It is revival or removal!

It is my sincere prayer that the contents of this book will "Light A Fire" in this country that will stir all America to go and get the freedoms the Devil has stolen! These stolen goods must be returned!

May the information on these pages inspire you to become a flame in the Revival Fires!

Cecil Todd
Director & President
Revival Fires Ministry
Joplin, MO 64801

Scenes like the above are common and so thrilling. More than 350,000 souls have made public decisions for Jesus Christ in the Revival Fires crusades and rallies. More than anything else, the Cecil Todd directed services are dedicated to reaching people for Christ and Eternity!

CHAPTER ONE

THE FIRES OF FREEDOM!

On Christmas Eve, 1968, the world stood at attention as Astronaut Frank Borman, flying in space, read from the Word of God.

He was permitted to carry only a few items on the space ship. His Bible was one of them! He opened the Word of God to the first page of the first book and, as the world listened, he read the first ten verses.

The passage he selected tells about, our Creator. It declares, "In the beginning, God created the heaven and the earth . . ." It tells how God reached forth with a torch of His omnipotence and set ablaze the sun . . . and it has never gone out since . . .

He flung the stars into space . . . more than our astronomers with their high power telescopes can count or even in their wildest dreams imagine.

He carved out the valleys and piled up the mountains and created the oceans, seas, and sent rivers and streams hunting for them.

He created it all . . . from the beautiful flowers on the sides, to the barren ice covered mountaintops.

Yes, our God made it all!

The crown of His creation was man. He formed Adam out of the dust of the earth and breathed into his nostrils the breath of life and man became a living soul.

As Frank Borman read this account from God's Word from his "pulpit" in space, the whole world was spellbound. From out in space came a voice of an astronaut looking down on the planet Earth and telling how our mighty God had made everything that any man could see.

What a testimony!

For almost 200 years, this was the very heart of America. This was what America was really like . . . and what America is supposed to be like today.

But are we? If Mr. Borman had done this today, what would the reaction be? Sadly, some Americans would not receive it so joyfully. Even then there was opposition from the atheists. The attack on God in America has been so strong that I doubt it would have been aired, and if it had been, the following days atheists and others would have marched and protested in our streets!

What has America come to? Where have our freedoms gone? And who is to blame? More important, how can we get them back?

Our country was built on freedom. When our Founding Fathers, the early pilgrims, came to this country, they came across the rough waters of the Atlantic, leaving behind loved ones, homelands, possessions and all they had ever owned.

They left civilization for a raw wilderness. They left their country to carve out a new land for one main reason . . . so they could worship God according to the dictates of their hearts and consciences!

The price they paid for that freedom . . . a freedom they were dedicated to passing on to generations to come . . . was dear . . . precious and priceless!

For days . . . weeks . . . and even months, they traveled the high seas in wooden ships barely surviving on the food and water that was allowed. Storms were known to swallow up whole vessels, yet they believed the risk was worth the reward!

I've read of how many of them, when they finally landed on the shores of this great nation, fell on their faces and thanked God and kissed the American soil.

That's how much America . . . even before it was named . . . meant to them. Even the soil stood for freedom.

How can we take it for granted?

Ask any of the hostages that were taken in Iran how they felt upon returning to America. Many of them also kissed the ground of America as soon as they came off the plane.

I have traveled overseas. My wife and I have gone overseas on several crusades and my teams and I have been on campaigns in fifty-five different countries around the world.

But I tell you, there is no place like America!

We may have our faults and our problems, but I'll shout it from the housetops, "This country is still the greatest nation in all the world! She is still worth fighting for! She is still worth praying for and defending!"

All you have to do is visit some of these other nations and you will readily see.

America was built on a solid foundation of the

Word of God. The first public buildings built were churches . . . and the Bible was a textbook in our first schools.

When they began to frame the Constitution, the Bill of Rights, the Declaration of Independence, and put together this nation of colonies, we are told tempers flared as our early leaders gathered in the Constitution Hall in Philadelphia.

Men frustrated in their own understanding were at the verge of verbal battle with each other over the wording of these great documents.

As the tempers exploded the delegates were ready to go back to their respective colonies unsuccessful in writing the Constitution. But, it was then that the great patriot by the name of Benjamin Franklin, called that first Continental Congress together and asked those men to get down upon their knees on the floor of the Constitution Hall and ask for God's guidance and God's help in the writing of the Constitution.

Those men responded to that request. They fell on their faces and prayed for God's help and wisdom. When they came up off their knees, they went on to write one of the greatest documents of all time in America, second only to the Bible, as far as I am concerned - The Constitution of the United States.

It was written after a prayer meeting by the delegates to that Constitutional Convention. It was after that when Benjamin Franklin and the others had left the Constitution Hall, a lady came up to Mr. Franklin and said, "Well, do we have a republic?" His reply was "classic." He said, "Yes, we have a republic, if we can hold it, if we can keep it!"

For more than two hundred years, that's what American patriotism has been all about - to "hold it!" What has been the cement - what has been the glue - that has done it? Well, you can see our military muscle and our legislative power. You can see our free enterprise and our ingenuity. All of these ingredients have their places. But, I tell you the glue that has held this country together from it's birth has been Almighty God!

The Bible was our Founding Father's guiding light . . . their road map to live by. It told them, and it tells us, how to live and how to die.

The Word of God is still the hope and the help for this hour and the Word of God is still the lamp unto our feet and the light unto our pathway. The axe . . . symbolic of hard work, sweat, blood, callouses and blisters. The gun . . . symbolic of protection and provision.

It was a black day in American history when the Supreme Court decided it was unlawful for prayer and Bible reading to be held in our public schools. Efforts have been made by countless groups across the land to get the Bible and prayer back into the public school and more of God and His power and His fire back into the pulpits and pews in our churches! Yes, this country of ours, needs a revival fire! There is nothing wrong in America, but what a good "Old Fashioned" Holy Ghost Revival wouldn't correct!

The historian, Roger Babson, said many years ago, "People went to South America in search of gold, but they came to North America in search of God."

I tell you God has been the very soul of this country from it's beginning. Only as we keep God as the heart of our country, of our homes and of our personal lives, are we going to survive as a nation!

But there are satanic forces at work to take God's power and influence out of our country . . . and out of our very lives!

They are working in every area, yes, even in our churches. There are many churches that are spiritually as dead as last year's bird's nest! They are so dignified and sophisticated that if somebody said, "Amen" or "Praise God" while the preacher was preaching, everybody would turn around to see who it was . . . and the preacher would probably lose his train of thought.

As our spiritual leadership and foundations are weakened in America . . . so is America itself.

We must once again ignite a spiritual fire in America. Something valuable and precious has been stolen from us. We know who did it and where they are and it is up to us, with the authority of Jesus Christ to go forth in His name of power and victory and recapture our stolen freedoms!

This, my friends, is what God has put upon my heart to tell you and tell all America . . . "Too many of our freedoms have been stolen . . . and it is our personal and Christian responsibility to get them back!

I ask that you do more than read this book; I ask you to study it. Through these pages you will begin to understand what is happening in America, in our seats of government, in our churches, and in our public schools.

If we are going to change this country we must first be on fire for God ourselves. You can only spread God's fire, if you are on fire! We can't expect to move our communities or our nation unless we have been moved.

This book is not designed to tickle your toes . . . it may peel your hide and nail it to the wall! I want to see every born-again Christian on the war path for God! Jesus Christ has declared war on sin and Satan . . . it's high time we got in the fight too . . . We must go forth and recapture our God given freedoms, stolen from us by the Devil's disciples!

Bill Murray, son of atheist Madalyn Murray O'Hair and Cecil Todd look again at II Chronicles 7:14 in the Word of God. After Bill was born again, he and Cecil teamed up to hold over seventy-five crusade rallies across America.

CHAPTER TWO

WHILE WE PLAYED, THE THIEVES STOLE OUR GOODS!

One of our most cherished freedoms . . . prayer in our public schools . . . has been stolen! Not revoked or repealed. The right to pray in public schools was forcibly stolen from millions of Americans by Satan and his dedicated followers!

For a nation built on religious freedom, proudly displaying the stars and stripes of Old Glory and bearing the motto "In God We Trust," there should be no place in our land, whether it be in the school house or the White House, where prayer and Bible reading is forbidden!

Yet almost weekly, stories appear in the newspaper of many freedoms of religious expression and exercise that are being stolen from us one by one.

How have our goods been stolen? Because we lost the fire and power of God! Even the fullness of the power that is available through the Holy Ghost in our churches, in our pulpits and in our pews seems to have waned. If we can get the fire and power of God back into our church, we will once again rise up like a mighty army and go out and recover the freedoms that have been stolen from us by the devil. This desperate hour demands our wholehearted commitment to the cause of Jesus Christ.

I believe it is the time for the Christians in America

to take a stand. Together, we can regain our stolen freedoms!

To understand the true horror of that landmark decision that has so molded this downward trend in our rights, by the High Court one can study William Murray's book *"My Life Without God."*

In this book, written after he was born-again, Bill shares about his tragic and traumatic childhood at the hands of a woman who showed no love or interest in her first-born illegitimate son.

Raised in a tiny house with his mother, grandparents and uncle, Bill was eight years old before he understood that "Madalyn" was his mother.

She became pregnant with Bill while she was overseas during World War II. Her lover, a Roman Catholic, refused to divorce his wife to marry her because of how the Church felt about divorce. Apparently his religion would allow him to commit adultery, but not to divorce his wife!

Nevertheless, she named the child after him, and at some point, added Murray to her own name, though no wedding ever took place, according to Bill's testimony.

He related that in the years that followed, his mother job-hopped every six months or so due to trouble with supervisors. Finally fed up with the American system, she tried unsuccessfully to defect to the Soviet Union, even after traveling all the way to France to speed the process!

Rejected and discouraged, she returned to America unwillingly and very bitter, according to Bill, and went to enroll him back in school shortly after their return. It was on that trip to school that she discovered the children praying. She declared, "If we can't live in the Soviet Union where all of this is forbidden, we must change this country where they can't do it here either!" Originally this anti-God and anti-Bible crusade had nothing to do with "Constitutional Rights" or "Separation of Church and State" but one woman's war against God, who had, in her opinion denied her the marriage to her lover!

Her deep-rooted anger against God, Church and America finally had an outlet, a cause, and within months, she almost single-handedly succeeded in stealing from America the right to pray in public schools.

Shock waves spread scross America as religious and government leaders from almost every level expressed sorrow and shock at the Supreme Court's 8-1 decision.

Satan had successfully used one person to bar the rights and desires of millions. All of a sudden, America dropped a notch from being the "land of the free." This freedom was stolen.

History plainly documents that this country was born on bended knees with an open Bible in our forefathers' hands!

It seems hardly possible that our nation, whose spiritual heritage has been so rich, would ever turn its back from the God who gave us life, liberty and a reason to live!

But the problem has not ended with the stolen freedom of prayer taken from our public schools. Many school officials have misinterpreted this decision of the High Court and have also stopped any celebration of Christmas, Easter, baccalaureate services and other programs that are so much a part of our rich spiritual heritage.

Groups of high school students are allowed to hold meetings on school grounds for studying yoga, witchcraft and satanism but Christians are banned from using school property for studying the Word of God. As students have told me, "We have rooms to smoke our cigarettes and to smoke our "pot" but we are denied rooms where we can pray and read our Bibles."

One such case was reported by the Associated Press:

> Washington (AP) - "The Supreme Court barred a group of public high school students Monday from using a vacant classroom for prayer meetings before class, and dealt a possibly serious blow to hundreds of thousands of Vietnam Veterans with claims against the makers of the defoliant Agent Orange.
> Action in the prayer case came just one week after the justices ruled that state colleges must allow student groups to worship and hold religious discussions in campus buildings if other student groups are allowed access."

But the Supreme Court consistently has treated public, elementary and secondary schools differently from state colleges and universities when it comes to religious matters.

Monday's action in a New York case, coupled with certain language in last week's decision involving the University of Missouri at Kansas City, appeared to preserve the distinction made between students of different ages.

Neither case gave any indication that the justices were about to reconsider their 1962 ban on organized prayer sessions in public elementary and secondary schools.

The justices, without comment, left intact rulings that barred early morning prayer meetings at Guilderland High School near Albany, N.Y.

Six Guilderland students sued the school board in 1979 after their group *Students For Voluntary Prayer,* was denied permission to meet in an unused classroom before the start of classes each day.

Other student groups routinely were granted permission for such unsupervised meetings.

The 2nd U.S. Circuit Court of Appeals in November, 1980 agreed that the school board unconstitutionally would have been advancing religion if it had granted the study group's request.

Here's more signs of the growing decay in our society, since prayer was forced out of the public schools:

* Bibles are being barred more and more from public schools.
* Bibles have been removed from the shelves in some school libraries.
* One million teen-age girls became pregnant in 1981 alone. 400,000 of these babies were aborted . . . murdered before they even had a chance at life.
* Almost 5,000 school children committed suicide in 1981.
* One hundred school children were murdered in the public schools last year.

* All but ten percent of the sixty million kids in our public schools have tried dope and drugs and many are "hooked" on it!

Yet an opportunity to teach godly morality has been stripped from concerned Christian teachers in the public schools!

Sometime ago, the U.S. Supreme Court ruled against Kentucky posting the Ten Commandments in the classrooms in the state.

Phi Delta Kappan quoted the attorney on the case, William Stone, as saying that this ruling may "serve as a warning to the (Christians) majority that they cannot impose their will simply because they out-number minority believers."

George Gallop surveys have revealed that up to 85% of the people favor voluntary prayer in the public schools. Why is it that in this country, that is recognized around the world as a democracy, that the 15% who oppose prayer in the public schools are having more influence than the 85% who favor it?

Apparently it is because the 15% opponents are making more noise, spending more time, giving more of their effort than we who comprise the 85%!

I believe it is high time that these noisy minorities quit dictating the policies for the whole country. If the people of God don't stand up and do something about this anti-God, anti-Christ, anti-Bible and anti-prayer movement, who will?

I am reminded of Paul's words to Timothy in I Timothy 6:12, "Fight on for God. Hold tightly to the eternal life which God has given you, and which you have confessed with such a ringing confession before many witnesses.''

You must . . . and I must, if we are to change the crash course America is on! Our country must once again become the government of the people . . . for the people, and by the people!

In a land where the majority rule has been one of the high standards of democracy, this whole problem seems so misplaced.

In Russia, less than five percent of the entire nation embrace Communism, yet those few dictate the policies of the entire Soviet Union.

Is this where America is heading? Or have we already arrived? Not yet, as far as I'm concerned, and I believe a multitude of other Americans share my same convictions!

The Christian people in Russia and other communistic nations are held back from freedom of worship by the threat of firing squads, slave camps, heavy fines and all types of oppression. I have heard them saying, ''When good men do nothing, men like Hitler come into power.'' Do we want that?

Most communistic countries became that way because good Christian people were so busy with church meetings and other things that they refused to get involved! They did not vote and they did not take a stand for God when it counted.

Then suddenly it was too late.

It is almost too late now for America, if Christians don't begin now to get involved, get informed and take a bold, courageous stand for the godly ways that made this country great!

These atheistic leaders will not be satisfied with just banning prayer and Bible reading from our public schools.

They are now mounting satanic attacks to get the words "In God We Trust" stricken from our coins and currency, all church property taxed, the removal of all chaplains from our armed services and the House and Senate, plus many other godless directions.

Freedom after freedom is being stolen away right before our very eyes. These moves toward an anti-God government brings America closer and closer to self-destruction! The enemy wants to win without firing a shot! President Lincoln said, "If we are defeated it will be from within."

Will you stand idly by and let this happen? Not Cecil Todd . . . it will be over my dead body!

Christians must become righteously indignant, stand up and take charge. We must carry our cause to the streets, to the courtrooms and to the ballot boxes to stop the stealing of our freedoms, our liberties and our desire to keep this country "one nation under God!"

If communism is so great, why do the governments denying God have to build such high fences around their borders to keep in their people. Why are soldiers posted at their boundaries with high-powered rifles and machine guns with orders to "shoot to kill" anyone who tries to escape over these fences or high walls?

Though it is only a small sympton of the real problem in Communist Russia, consider their agricultural situation.

In the Russian Revolution the state seized more than 98% of Russia's land that was used for farming. To do this Communists killed many of the land owners or sent them to prison camps in Siberia. Then the state took over the farms, keeping the profit for Kremlin use. Only 1.6% of the land was left in the hands of private citizens.

The 1.6% owned privately produces 64% of Russia's potatoes, 35% of the milk, 50% of the eggs and 35% of the meat. Half of all the agricultural products produced in Russia overall are produced by the 1.6% of the land that belongs to individuals!

I believe this is a prime example of the fruits of freedom. The free land, whether that 1.6% in Russia, or America itself, where there is no freedom, there is nothing. Even the desire to live is lost!

In many areas of America, students are praying despite the Court's ruling. One school in Rapides Parish, LA was so bold, we ran an article about it in an issue of Revival Fires.

Today, America stands at the crossroads with one foot already headed down the highway of self-destruction!

A Gallup Poll showed that 84% of Americans claim to believe the Ten Commandments are of God, and are valid today; however, more than 50% of them couldn't even recall five of them.

It's time for America to wake up or break-up! It's time for the people of God to be used to shake this country and turn it around for Jesus Christ . . . NOW!

Our generation has grown fat and sleek in its soul! We are accustomed to going to church and hearing soft, warmed-over platitudes. What we need is a stick of spiritual dynamite to blast us out of these ruts of apathy, self-righteousness and complacency and on to God's highway of holiness and service.

Christ-haters and Bible-debunkers have swarmed from their hideouts and have launched the most merciless attack upon God, His Word and prayer that has ever been. It is high time that the people of God came from their seats to their feet and into the streets in the name of the Lord God Jehovah. Our Lord has promised that as we go, "Lo, I am with you!"

Most people think that one person can't change anything. But look at what Madalyn Murray O'Hair did all by herself.

We, as Christians, have more power than she and all the demons of hell, for we have the Creator of the universe on our side!

This book contains some frightening facts; facts that will send chills down your spine, but it also holds the answer to the problem . . . answers only in the hands of the people of God!

Jesus said, "I want you to be the light and salt of the earth." I know we, as Christians, are just "passing through" and Jesus is coming soon, but He also said, "Occupy til I come." We must be the salt and light in our communities. Light drives darkness away and salt flavors and preserves both food and nations. That is why it is important that we be the "salt" and the "light" in this dark and sin-rottening hour!

CHAPTER THREE

THE HIGH PRICE OF PLAYING!

It was 200 years ago that Edmund Burke said, "The only thing necessary for evil to triumph is for good men to do nothing."

Although over two hundred years old, these words speak with meaning for today. The truth of it is echoed by national leaders and concerned patriots across America. America truly stands at the crossroads. In fact, there are many who say we have already gone too far down the road of lust, liquor and license, infidelity and drunkenness, to turn back!

We have gone too far to be saved by human ingenuity . . .

The only thing that can save us now is the intervention of the divine hand of Almighty God!

I believe America is facing a big decision. God's Word has a word of warning for this hour; the nation of Israel is an example for us. Moses said in Deuteronomy 30:19: "I call heaven and earth to record this day against you, that I have set before you life and death, blessing and cursing; therefore, choose life, that both thou and thy seed may live."

These words spoken by Moses to the nation of Israel, also speak to us. We, too, are faced with the choice of life or death as individuals and as a nation!

America has begun to pay the price for taking God out of our public schools. God offers us as a nation, life or death. But which have we chosen? Only as we choose God, His ways and His Word, do we choose life!

First of all, consider what God says about death. Our lawlessness, our sin and disobedience have spelled death for us.

Another prophet said in Ezekiel 18:4: "The soul that sinneth it shall die." This is the law of the harvest, and God is not mocked! The apostle Paul, with the pen of the Spirit, put it in these words, "For the wages of sin is death; but the gift of God is eternal life through Jesus Christ our Lord." (Romans 6:23) Death is the payment for sin . . . for men and nations! Let it thunder in your soul - you cannot sin and get away with it! Nobody can! Most Americans have chosen the path of death. Most Americans have chosen the pleasures of the world over service to Christ. We have chosen material things over spiritual opportunities. Most Americans prefer to fill the beaches, picnic areas, parks and our congested highways on the Lord's Day. We are running, racing headlong down the highway to death! We have chosen the television over the Trinity, Hollywood over Heaven and we have chosen death and not life!

This has happened in our homes. So many homes have chosen death. The enormous divorce rate is tragic. The national average is one divorce for every two marriages. In Hollywood and southern California, I'm told there are more divorces than there are marriages! Just fifty years ago there was one divorce for every thirty marriages. Today it is one out of every two marriages ending in the horrible divorce courts. Our homes have chosen death! The home is broken because of incompatibility, infidelity and lack of communication. You can spell them all with one small three lettered word . . . S-I-N!

What has happened? Numberless girls have had illegitimate children and abortions. Look what is happening on our college campuses. It is a well-known practice for boys and girls to share the same apartment and the same bed. Yes, our nation has chosen death rather than life in the home and in the school! How tragic, but how true.

Choosing death is not only true in the home, but it is increasingly true in our schools, colleges and universities.

The prayer issue is but one example. In the average school today, the theory of evolution, atheism, communism and secular humanism is taught in our classrooms.

Many teachers in our colleges do not believe the Bible any more! They even mock the Word of God! It is called a book of folklore, legend and stories handed down across the years. There are many teachers who sneeringly tell their students they are atheists. Such teachers often use profane language and set bad examples before the students. Think of it . . . a God to cuss by, but no God to pray to! And yet, in our schools the Bible and prayer are considered unconstitutional and unlawful. In most of jour public schools we have chosen death!

We have chosen death in many of our churches. Most churches are so worldly, you would have to backslide to have fellowship with them! Most preachers make Judas Iscariot look like an angel! Too many pastors are popular for what they do not believe. Modernism has killed faith. Compromise and experience have shut the mouth of preachers so you never hear about Jesus. Pomp and ceremony, traditions and doctrines of men have taken the place of "Thus saith the Lord!" In many churches, basements have been turned into sock-hops and disco parties. Many churches desecrate the platform with nudity and blasphemy! Homosexuals and other sex perverts are united in marriage in some so-called "churches!" All of this godlessness and abomination before God is going on in the name of religion in many church buildings. God have mercy!

But there is still a remnant, there are still those churches where God is honored, His name is praised, and the Bible is preached. There are still Christians whose faith is stronger than ever and who live lives of purity and holiness. There are still many people dedicated and separated from the world into Christ.

Yes, many preachers have forsaken the faith and deny our God as a God of miracles and power for today. But I tell you there are also many preachers who still have enough cement in their backbone and sand in their craws to boldly stand on their hind legs and call sin by its first name.

These men are willing, at the price of their own job, to point people to Jesus Christ as the only hope, and call people to repentance. These are God's spokesmen with words of warning to a nation that is traveling the highway to hell.

There is a price to pay for our liberated new concept of today that allows politicians and special minority groups to run the country in total disregard for the values and traditions held by the majority of Americans.

The quality of education has had a decline in high school standards. An article in *Time,* January 11, 1982, reported that: "State Universities try to cut the cost of failure" in which millions of dollars are spent on remedial courses for students not prepared to enter college - the following article revealed that between 1977-1980 only 25,000 students could demonstrate reading and writing skills necessary for college-level courses:

". . . U.C. Administrator Henry Alder stresses that low performance in high school could prove hazardous to college aspirations . . . the other cost is in the misdirection of talents in teaching." While some remedial programs hire specially trained teachers, many untenured and frustrated PHD's find themselves teaching Basic Reading and Algebra I rather than Literature or Calculus. Adds California State University Chancellor Glenn Dumke: "either the state university will direct its energy to the full meaning of 'higher education' or its campuses will continue being made into centers of remediation . . ."

The article further stated:

". . . Most of the problem, however, lies with past teen-age attitudes toward learning and a decade-long decline in high school standards. Wayne Brown of the Tennessee Higher Education Commission believes that the one million spent in his state on college remediation should be recycled into high school programs . . ."

With the quality of education down and the problem with past teen-age attitudes toward learning, there has become a vast number of dropouts from school. There are reportedly more than 800,000 school dropouts between the ages of 14 and 17 in the United States. Many of these children can barely read or write and are considered to be on the borderline of being illiterate.

Many of these children are confronted with a life of crime, drugs and even prostitution at an early age.

In the October, 1981 issue of Time, a story was presented of the life of a 14-year old boy in Brooklyn that is facing the cruel world of hopelessness offered by our society. The story is how some of the children in our country, described to us as a land of "milk and honey," are trapped by illiteracy and ignorance.

The subject lived on the fourth floor of a crumbling turn-of-the-century tenement with his Aunt located in Brooklyn's Bedford Stuyvesant section. It has the highest murder rate in Brooklyn with 86 killings last year.

He inhabited a world that few of us ever see - cheap thrills, senseless deaths, drugs and almost unrelieved hopelessness. He was 13 the first time he saw a man blown away - with a shotgun. He has experienced a few gunslingers himself with his .25 automatic that he sometimes carries.

Youngsters are among those who are killed on summer evenings when tough, mean young men shoot it out like the old western movies on TV. The dead are dumped in trashed buildings. Even some of his friends did not escape senseless deaths during the summer.

Friday nights are the big nights for gambling up and down the streets while the smell of marijuana fills the air. A born hustler, he is slick at pool and dice. He is one of the many that gamble on Friday nights with men who feed him a Puerto Rican, expecially potent, kind of marijuana. Up the block, twelve year old hookers parade around on high heels.

When he returns home he sleeps on a stained mattress in a small room shared with his cousins and an army of cockroaches.

He is trapped. He can barely read or write even though he would have been in the seventh grade this year. Because he is nearly illiterate, he could never hold even the most menial job for long. He has been running wild so long now that he may be beyond redemption. Ghetto children today are seduced much earlier by drugs on the street, and some of them are as young as eight or nine. It is incredible . . . almost too hard for most of us to even comprehend!

In this story it is revealed once again the wages of sin is death. This is a sad story of such young children at an age when they should be enjoying life to its fullest, not encountering drugs, prostitution and even death . . . the price is too high to pay. These children need the direction of a moral, godly society . . . in the schools and in the churches!

It is no wonder that our children are turning to such perversions with the media, television programs, ERA, proabortion and so on that is in the limelight so much in our country. Even teen-age record albums promote sex, violence, satanism and suicide. There is strong evidence of some record albums carrying messages to the subconscious mind when played backward. *Christian Life* reported that a Congressman proposed Satan record warnings in which it stated:

If Rep. Robert K. Dornan (R-Calif.) has

his way, Congress will require some record albums to carry warning labels. A bill Dornan recently introduced would require message, "Warning: These records contain background masking that makes a verbal statement which is audible when the record is played backward."

Dornan's bill comes amidst controversy concerning the importance of this issue. Since most turntables rotate only clockwise under power, the Satan messages some claim to hear on secular albums are "masked" from ordinary listeners. The messages can be heard only by manually rotating the turntable counter-clockwise - a maneuver which one recording company spokesman warned would ruin the machine. Others question the charge that such backward messages can even be heard subconsciously.

Robert Nolte, Director of Public Relations for Maranatha Campus Ministries, a ministry designed reach university students, researcheed this satanic influence.

In an article he wrote. ". . . California State Assemblyman, Phil Wyman, says hidden messages in rock 'n' roll music can manipulate our behavior without our knowledge or consent and turn us into disciples of the anti-Christ." Wyman, of Tehachapi, California, introduced the bill which is presently being studied by a consumer protection committee."

Nolte further documented, "Campus evangelist, Nick Pappis, says subliminal messages are introduced into rock 'n' roll music by using a technique called "back masking" first used in the mid-60's by the Beatles."

"Pappis, a traveling preacher with Maranatha Campus Ministries, says, 'Artists using back masking simply record a message backward and introduce it into their music, causing it to be indecipherable unless the record or tape is played backwards . . .'

". . . Pappis says, 'A Colorado researcher discovered that the subconscious mind can decipher the backward messages even when the record is played forward at normal speed. The researcher, William Yarroll of Applied Potential Institute in Aurora, Colorado, testified before the California investigative committee and has published papers on his findings. Yarroll said that in his research at the University of Colorado Health Science Center in Denver, he found some of the backward phrases from the rock records repeated in suicide notes penned by young people.'''

"Maranatha evangelists, Pappis and Holmberg, have gathered notebooks full of backward masking messages. Here are a few of them:

☆ On the Black Oak Arkansas song, "When Electricity Came to Arkansas," which was recorded live, a strange segment of the song features unintelligible words and howling sounds made by all the members. When this portion of the song is played backward, the message is, "Satan. Satan. Satan. He is god. He is god. He is god." and the message is completed with sickly laughter.

☆ Led Zeppelin's "Stairway to Heaven," one of the most popular rock 'n' roll song of all times, features lyrics which say, "There's still time to change the road you're on." When played backwards, that message is; "My sweet Satan, no other made a path; for it makes me sad, whose power is Satan."

☆ On the song, "Anthem," by Rush, the backwards message says, "Oh Satan, you are the one who is shining. Walls of Satan you are so sensuous. I know that you are the one I love."

☆ On Queen's Killers album, the title phrase of their song, "Another One Bites the Dust," when played backwards, says plainly, "Start to smoke marijuana . . . Satan must have no limits, no limit at all."

Wyman is calling for a joint hearing of the California Assembly constitutional amendments committee, of which he is chairman, and the consumer protection committee to fully investigate subliminal messages contained in records and tapes.

"One of the things we want to find out is why these messages are placed on records in the first place," said Wyman. "Exactly what is their purpose?"

Researcher Yarroll believes he may have the answer. During the California hearings, he said that a man from an organization calling itself the Church of Satan, called him after a television show in which he exposed rock music, warning him not to pursue his research. The TV show was broadcast nationwide by the Trinity Network of Santa Ana, California.

Yarrol said that rock artists add backward masking tracks to their records because, "the Church of Satan and their followers have a pact, that if you perform certain things in your particular line of work, in return Satan will give you certain favors back."

This trick of Satan is not new.

Even in the murder case of Charles Manson, he

made a statement in which he claimed to receive messages from Satan from the Beatles' record, "Helter, Skelter." Charles Manson and his followers brutally murdered Sharon Tate, an actress that was seven months pregnant at the time of her death in 1969.

Crime and murder are on the increase among our youth. Our youth have become adulterers and murderers . . . their hearts and minds have become calloused and insensitive. They live in a society that promotes, "If it feels good, do it." More and more cases are reported, as in the following report in *Time* magazine:

Until now the U.S. Supreme Court has not set maximum limits on the punishment of youthful criminals. But the Court is currently contemplating a juvenile death penalty case.

In Vermont, two boys, age 15 and 16, allegedly raped, stabbed and beat two twelve-year-old girls, killing one; an outraged legislature swiftly lowered the age in which a person may be tried and sentenced as an adult. The new age limit in Vermont is ten years old.

In Milpitas, California, teen-aged, Anthony Jacques, invited his friends out to see the body of his former girl-friend in which he braggingly told of strangling her.

Should the alleged killer be tried as a juvenile or as an adult? It is a question that is increasingly posed by a society that has become terrified of its young.

In Texas, David Keeler shot to death his mother and father. When David reaches the age of 18, he will no longer be under the control of juvenile officials.

Last March in California, two boys aged

17, who raped and attempted to murder a young woman, were each sentenced by an adult court, to 72 years to life in prison without parole until they are 65.

In 1977, a sawed-off shotgun was used when Monty Lee Eddings, then 16, murdered an Oklahoma Highway Patrolman. He was condemned to death by an adult court. However the court rules, the public mood apparently holds that anyone old enough to commit the crime is old enough to pay the price.

The cliche, "What you see, is what you get" is a common saying in our society. This is true in viewing what our media and television programming brings into our homes. We see murder, theft, immorality and witchcraft. We see it as the right way or the "in" thing for our contemporary society of today rather than against our traditional moral and godly standards that are the foundation formulated by God.

X-rated, R-rated and pornographic movies are on the increase because the general public is beginning to believe that "no one should be able to tell me what I can watch, read or publish."

It is a noted fact that some men who hang around pornographic movies often become so stimulated they go out and rape innocent victims or expose themselves to little children on school playgrounds.

Even in the recent attempt of John Hinckley's shooting of President Reagan, it was brought to everyone's attention that he was provoked to do it by a movie he had seen and became obsessed with. There was the question concerning John Hinckley's sanity in which it was stated that he was so phychologically troubled when he shot President Reagan and three other men that society questioned his accountability for his actions.

This insanity hogwash has allowed too many criminals, rapists and murderers to go free. In my opinion, if they are sane enough to commit the crime, they are sane enough to pay the penalty!

Also the openness concerning sex and immorality brings more and more attention to pregnancy and abortion. Since 1973, the biological holocaust of abortion has taken the lives of some ten to fifteen million little unborn babies. This is even worse than the Nazi holocaust under Adolph Hitler during World War II. What makes it wrong for Hitler to kill six million Jews, but not so wrong for ten million mothers in cooperation with their doctors to murder their unborn babies?

There is a price to pay for murder and immorality that our nation must pay . . . our responsibility began with our youth, as the Scripture in Proverbs 22:6 says, "Train up a child in the way he should go; and when he is old, he will not depart from it." We, as adults, have a responsibility to ourselves as well. Jerry Falwell said:

Americans must no longer linger in ignorance and apathy. We cannot be silent about these sins that are destroying this nation. The choice is ours. We must turn America around or prepare for inevitable destruction."

There may be times when silence is golden, but this is not that time . . . Silence can be downright yellow!

Some may cry out, "But you can't legislate morality!" I agree one thousand per cent! But why don't our lawmakers stop legislating immorality!

CHAPTER FOUR

FROM GOO TO YOU BY
WAY OF THE ZOO

"In the beginning, God created the heaven and the earth." Genesis 1:1 . . . .

A lot of people today don't believe that such a living God exists, as is obvious by our nation's and school's conditions.

Enemies of the Gospel explain everything in existence as the result of a slow process that developed man from monkeys. Then they say some slime collected and eventually, animals and man crawled out of it . . . "From goo to you by way of the zoo," as Harold Hill put it.

These thoughts aren't new. Isaac Newton, the scientist who discovered the Law of Gravity once had a visitor who looked at a model of the solar system in Newton's lab and asked, "Who made that model?"

"Nobody," Newton replied.

"What kind of fool do you take me for, this is the work of a genius," the man stated sharply.

Newton reached out to touch the globe. "It is only a poor imitation of a much greater system," he said. "How is it that I cannot convince you that this didn't have a designer or maker?"

The Bible talked about these kind of men:

"Professing themselves to be wise, they became fools, and changed the glory of the incorruptible God into an image made like to corruptible man, and to birds, and four-footed beasts and creeping things." Romans 1:22-23

Did you know that Charles Darwin, the naturalist who made popular the theory of evolution, met the Lord before he died and repudiated his controversial theory? It's true! I would to God our news media would report this . . . and that our school kids were told the whole truth about Charles Darwin. The Devil is such a deceiver and liar!

According to Darwin's early theory, man evolved from lower forms of life. As the theory of evolution took hold of men's minds, many gladly accepted it as fact and as a way to prove that God's Word was untrue. History has shown again and again that there are no limits to what ungodly men will go, to try and discredit the Bible and to justify their sins! We have made a god out of ungodly science, and begun to worship man's wisdom just as in Paul's description in the above verse. They then forced it on our children in public schools.

There is a great debate in our country concerning the subject of Biblical Creation vs. The Theory of Evolution, a theory quite different for most children who grew up in a home believing in a Supreme Being creating the earth and everything in it.

The Evolution Theory is taught in our schools all over our country from the first grade on.

Bill Keith in his book "Scopes II The Great Debate" tells of a personal account from Attorney

Wendell Bird of the great influence evolutionary teaching can have on a young mind.

Bird said he enrolled in a public school biology class in the tenth grade. The textbook said that life came about and developed through evolution and did not mention any alternative view.

His teacher assured him that evolution was the most reasonable explanation of our origins and that all scientists believe it.

Bird did not have a background or learning in the subject of creation and greatly respected the knowledge of his teacher. He learned evolution in biology, chemistry, world history, social studies and anthropology. The result was that he came to believe in "Theistic Evolution" and never knew that many scientists believed another viewpoint.

Wendell Bird later became a talented young scientist, winning third place in the International Science Fair for a project in biology. He was also named one of the top 40 young scientists in the land by a Westinghouse Science Talent Search. But all during that time he never heard there was a scientific alternative to evolution.

Bird's experience is repeated in the lives of tens of millions of young people who enter public schools. Yet, unlike Bird, millions of them begin the school year believing in creation and then, when confronted with evolution, are never told that it is unproven.

Bill Keith is very enlightening in describing evolution as pure humanism. He continues to add that a very wise man once described secular humanism as "human ego and intelligence gone mad."

Those who embrace this religion try to make a man out of the Creator and a creator out of man. They say there is no such thing as a Creator, that the idea was devised by man. In other words, the Creator didn't create man - man created the Creator. Their faith is in man and no one else.

Experts who study the religion of secular humanism estimate that there are fewer than 300,000 hard core humanists in this country. But millions believe in some of the tenets of humanism and tens of millions are being influenced by their religion every day.

Though limited in numbers, their influence is far-reaching and permeates every facet of society. For instance, they:

☆ Control public education in America Today.

☆ Wield a strong influence on the news media.

☆ Influence most all textbooks used in our public schools.

☆ Dominate many areas of state and federal government, particularly the programs governmental bodies carry out.

Their humanistic doctrines are flooding this country today. It has a terrifying impact on the people in general and school children in particular.

The U.S. Supreme Court (Torcaso vs. Watkins, 1961, and United States vs. Seeger, 1964) declared that humanism meets all the criteria for a bonafide religion.

Mel and Norma Gabler of Longview, Texas, have

studied secular humanism for many years. The following is based on their findings. Most of the teachings come directly from Humanist Manifestos I and II, the humanist's bible.

1.   EVOLUTIONARY DOGMA. Humanists falsely state that it is a scientific fact, rather than a theory.

2.   SELF AUTONOMY. This is the belief that there is no higher authority and therefore everyone, including children, must become their own authorities.

3.   SITUATION ETHICS. This concept teaches that nothing is absolutely right or wrong and that everything is situational or relative.

4.   CHRISTIANITY IS PASSE. It negates Christianity and all reference to the supernatural.

5.   SEXUAL FREEDOM. This idea provides the impetus for public sex education - but with no moral teaching included. It makes fun of modesty, purity, chastity and abstinence. It encourages abortion, pre-marital sex and homosexuality.

6.   TOTAL READING FREEDOM. They believe children should have the right to read anything and everything and that parents should not be a part of the decision-making process.

7.   DEATH EDUCATION. This concept teaches there is no life beyond the grave.

8.   INTERNATIONALISM. World citizenship, according to humanists, is far superior to national citizenship, patriotism and love for country.

9.   SOCIALISM. They believe that state ownership of property is far superior to private ownership.

This man-made religion is particularly widespread in public school textbooks.

Textbooks dealing with evolution teach that man is just an animal with no soul. Let's look at several examples:

"...Infants can grasp an object such as a finger so strongly that they can be lifted into the air. We suspect this reflex is left over from an earlier age in human evolution, when babies had to cling to their ape-like mother's coats while mothers were climbing or searching for food." *Understanding Psychology,* Random House.

"Man is, without question, the most outstanding product of evolution.

In a sense, human evolution has been in process since the first stirrings of life on earth." *BSCB Molecules to Man,* Houghton-Miffin.

This is puré speculation based on evolutionary, humanistic faith. Since they deny the existence of a Creator, they try to fit scientific data into their own presupposition that all things evolved - molecule to man.

Now let's look at text book examples of the belief in self-autonomy. This is the idea that man is just an animal and responsible to no one.

"The place, the opportunity, and their bodies all said, 'Go!'; How far this couple goes must be their own decision." *Masculinity and Feminity,* Houghton-Miffin.

This teaching is directly opposed to the teaching most children learn in the home.

From whom might you resent getting some unasked-for advise about how to dress, how to wear make-up, or how to behave? Why? (From some teachers, from 'old-fashioned' parents, from bossy older brothers and sisters). *Rebels and Regulars,* Teachers Manual, MacMillan.

Do you see the irony in this kind of teaching?

Parents and you, through your taxes, construct school buildings, purchase textbooks and pay teachers' salaries. Yet often the textual material attempts to undercut parental authority, and your personal desires. What about situation ethics?

"There are exceptions to almost all moral laws, depending on the situation. What is wrong in one instance may be right in another. Most children learn that it's tactless, if not actually wrong, not to lie under certain circumstances." *Inquiries in Sociology,* Allyn & Bacon.

Here's another example:

"Note (to teacher): Please refrain from moralizing of any kind. Students may indeed 'tune out' if they are subjected to "preachy' talk about 'proper English' and the moral obligation to 'do one's best' in class and to 'lend a hand' to the underdog in a battle . . ." *Gateway English,* MacMillan.

How does secular humanism negate traditional teaching of Judeo-Christian belief on which this nation was founded?

"Anthropologists studying human customs, religious practices, ritualism, and the priest craft came to the conclusion that men created their own religious beliefs so that the beliefs answered their special needs. The God of Judeo-Christian tradition was a god worshipped by a desert folk . . . and heaven was high above the desert . . . *Perspective in U.S. History,* Field Education Publications.

This is a frontal attack on the beliefs they learned in the home.

Why is such a blatant attack on the beliefs of the children necessary? Because the humanists must destroy all other religions for their own religion to thrive and capture the minds of all the people.

The Humanist Manifesto says: "Traditional theism, expecially faith in the prayer-hearing God, assumed to love and care for persons, to hear and understand their prayers and to be able to do something about them is an unproved and outmoded faith. Salvationism, based on mere affirmation, still appears as harmful, diverting people with false hopes of heaven hereafter. Reasonable minds look to other means for survival."

Here's another example of how humanism attempts to destroy other systems:

"A great many myths deal with the idea of rebirth. Jesus, Dionysus, Odin and many other traditional figures are represented as having died, after which they were reborn, or arose from the dead . . ." *Psychology for You,* Oxford.

These textbooks, written by humanistic writers, offer no alternative views other than humanism. Other views are not tolerated.

What do humanists teach about sexual freedom?

Here's what they believe and teach your children:

> "There are some who adopt more permissive standards for themselves and others. They propose conditions outside of marriage under which they feel that sexual relations should be permitted." *Psychology for Living,* Webster/McGraw.

Opinion polls reveal that most Americans still believe sex outside of marriage is wrong. So why is it being presented to school children as right and acceptable? It's plain to see for those who want to see . . . Satan has blinded their eyes and sin has darkened their minds to the truth of God and His Holy Word!

Humanists recommend total reading freedom for children. Perhaps that's why school libraries have so many books on witchcraft, black magic and the occult.

Here's what the Humanist Magazine said about reading freedom:

> "Something wonderful, free, unheralded and of significance to all humanists is happening in the secondary schools. It is the adolescent literature movement. They burned "Slaughterhouse Five" in North Dakota and banned a number of books in Kanaway County, but thank God, the crazies don't do all that much reading.

If they did, they'd find that they have already been defeated. Adolescent literature has opened a Pandora's Box . . . Nothing that is a part of contemporary life is taboo in this genre, and any valid piece of writing that helps to make the world more knowable to young people serves as important humanistic function."

Humanists have outsmarted parents. While most parents watched their TV's and made their money, and fulfilled their fleshly lusts, humanists were busy re-writing school textbooks which struck at the very heart of the beliefs most parents had instilled in their children. Sad to say, most parents have never even looked at the school textbooks being studied by their children. And for some strange reason (planned?), most school kids don't bring their textbooks home for study anymore. I'm convinced we have a satanic conspiracy in action, as the secular humanists vie for the minds of our young people.

In the meantime, the news media also spreads Humanistic beliefs throughout the country. Everyone is aware of the vast power that the media and television have in America. Reporters are allowed to include their own idea and view on most of the subjects reported. It is evident in the negative reports that people in the media no longer support objectively what the majority of the public want, which are articles based only on facts.

The American Civil Liberties Union (ACLU) is the legal arm of secular humanism in our culture. It is a very powerful organization which works continually on behalf of radical causes. They are opposed to the following concerns that are a vital part of our religion and heritage as God-fearing Americans and Christians!

- Voluntary prayer in schools and other public bodies.
- Equal time for creation - science in public schools.
- Displays of manger scenes at Christmas time in any public building.
- Laws which strengthen the police to help bring law and order to our society.
- The Congressional Committee on Un-american activities, the official committee charged with investigation of Communist Acts of conspiracy in this country.

The causes ACLU support are:

- ☆ The right for people to burn the American flag and draft cards and to dodge the draft.
- ☆ The right for a woman to have an abortion, thus murdering helpless, defenseless, harmless unborn babies.
- ☆ The right for porno-producers to distribute all forms of pornography.
- ☆ The right for Nazis to march in Skokie, Illinois, regardless of how the majority of the townspeople felt about it.
- ☆ The right of Communists and Communist-front organizations to advocate the overthrow of democracy in America.
- ☆ The right of Marxist professors to teach Marxism in taxpayer-supported state universities.
- ☆ The right of illegal aliens to come to the United States and take jobs away from American workers.
- ☆ The total freedom for all kinds of gambling.

It is time for us to wake up and realize just what our children are being taught . . . and to do something about getting God back in our classrooms. It's plain to see; since God has been expelled from our public schools, the Devil and his disciples have had a holiday!

The only "liberties" the American Civil Liberties Union wants to protect are those of prostitutes, draft dodgers, Nazis, Communists, atheists and Pornographers. They are powerful in defending freedom of *their* speech, but not yours.

The ACLU had been at the forefront of destroying our youth beginning with abortions. Their goal is in opposing democracy where the will of the majority is supposed to prevail in all matters. They realize that a country cannot last in which the murder of its unborn infants is freely allowed.

The ACLU has always favored draft dodgers and flag burners, thus keeping their secular humanism philosophy to turn our nation around to socialistic principles. In order to turn our country around they must change the attitude of the people and their loce for their country, their flag and traditional moral standards. Unless they accomplish this change in attitude, they will never witness our nation's downfall

The "Review of the News" wrote an account on Foundering ACLU, Roger Baldwin's camouflage patriotism -

> The ACLU disguise of patriotic concern for America's Constitution and our civil liberties is beginning to wear thin. Americans with well developed moral sensibilities

fail to see how the cause of freedom is to be served by abolishing the internal security laws of this nation, prohibiting capital punishment, legalizing abortion, destroying anti-obscenity laws, supporting a grape boycott, legalizing marijuana and other drugs, defending flag burning as a symbolic expression of free speech protected by the First Amendment, suing school officials for allegedly violating the Constitution by permitting the display of nativity scenes at Christmas, prohibiting children from praying at school, or supporting the so-called 'rights' of sex perverts to hold government jobs, teach school, and serve in the Armed Forces.

It is easy to agree with J.B. Matthews, longtime chief investigator of the House Special Committee on Un-American Activities, who observed in January, 1955: 'In thirty-seven years of history of the Communist movement in the United States, the Communist Party has never been able to do as much for itself as the American Civil Liberties Union had done for it.' The game is as insidious as it is simple. The 1966 Report of the Counter-Subversive Committee of the National Conference of Police Associations put it this way: 'In our opinion, the ACLU and its brother organizations have mastered the technique of Joseph Goebbels which is practiced by Moscow Communists to the nth degree. 'Tell a lie, make it big and tell it often enough so that soon everyone will believe it.'''

While Americans are watching their ball games,

playing video games and "doing their own thing," our traditional freedoms are being swept out from under us. Unless we, as Americans, wake up soon, our cherished freedoms, which were established in the beginning of our great nation, will be just a memory of "the good old days."

Our country is being demoralized. Sex appeal is advertised all the way from the selling of toothpaste to alcoholic beverages. The human body has become a "sex-symbol" and is causing a trend toward a sex-perverted society.

Many cities and nations of the past have been swept into ruin because of immorality - Sodom and Gomorrah, Babylon, Rome, Pompeii and others. Someone has said that the god of America is materialism and the goddess is sex.

Any nation that turns its back on God, or any nation that tramples His laws under its feet, is headed for chaos and judgment. History records the fall of twenty-one different civilizations. One thing can be found missing in each nation before its fall . . . its allegiance to Almighty God is gone. When a nation's spiritual backbone is broken, it's death certificate has been signed! What is true of a nation is just as true with an individual!

We spend four times as much money on pleasures, entertainment and amusement than we spend on all benevolent and charitable organizations combined. Jesus said, "Where you treasure is, there will your heart be also." (Matthew 6:21).

Our beaches are crowded, our highways are jammed, our woods are filled; picnics and sports seem to be the order of the day for most people. Most people are living to fulfill their own fleshly appetites. As the scripture says, ''They are lovers of pleasure more than lovers of God.'' (II Timothy 3:4).

Consider the great problems on our college campuses, with militant minorities wanting their way - girls and boys sharing the same dormitories, apartment houses, bedrooms, bearing illegitimate children proudly and having sex openly. They are all seekers of pleasures more than seekers of the will of God. They want no rules, no curfews and no laws. How can God bless America until America repents of this permissive, sinful, ''everything goes'' life-style.

Most real homes today are falling apart. Homes are being replaced with four walls. Children are left with the TV as their babysitter and to run wild on the streets!

Our ''Enemies,'' the thieves of Satan have stolen our freedoms! These demon-driven puppets of the Devil are organized and informed, dedicated and determined! Make no mistake about that!

The Devil's disciples are counting on the Christians to sit dumbly back and not get involved so they can push on to victory.

Yes, silence is not always golden . . . it can be downright yellow! And yes, the only thing necessary for evil to triumph is for good people to do nothing. The wages of sin is ... death ... for men and nations!

But let us consider . . .

Cecil and Linda were especially honored to be invited to join President Reagan for a short visit on Air Force One.

CHAPTER FIVE

THE THIEVES STOLE OUR KIDS!

After reading some of the figures in this book, or watching your local television station detail crimes at the hands of our youth, it may be easy to ask, "Is it worth it? Are these kids worth saving?"

The answer is a resounding "Yes!" The fact is the bad kids always get the news coverage. I believe the majority of the kids in America are good, God-fearing young people, hungry for God.

That is why our fight to get prayer back in the public school is so important.

This article was printed in "The Born-Again Christian Catalog," and was written by George Gallup, Jr.:

> "The shape of religion in America in the 1980's will in large measure be determined by the developing religious beliefs and practices of America's 25 million teenagers.
>
> Through the Gallup Youth Survey, it is now possible to test, on an ongoing basis, the religious viewpoints of this segment of the population.
>
> It is important for our churches to make strenuous efforts to reach the teenage population since many (in fact, half of high school graduates) will go on to college and

will therefore be subject to the secularizing effects of college.

Before young people enter college, they are a highly religious segment of our population, despite the commonly held belief that the teen-age years are in a period of religious doubt and skepticism.

An extraordinarily high proportion of teen-agers say they believe in God or a "personal" God who observes one's actions and rewards or punishes. Nearly nine in ten say they pray. Only one teen-ager in each one hundred says he or she has no religious preference or affiliation. The idea of going on religious "retreats" appeals to a surprising number of teen-agers.

The religious character of American youth stands out sharply when compared with that of youth in other major industrialized nations of the world. Gallup International surveys have indicated that levels of religious belief and practice in the United States are far higher and American teen-agers among the best church-goers.

The fact is, youth appear willing and eager to serve. This plus their deep-seated desire for meaningful religious experience presents a unique opportunity for the churches of America."

Yet we are not allowed to feed this hunger in a classroom setting, instead, just the opposite is promoted and encouraged. The story is told of a teacher who entered a classroom and saw a group of boys huddled in a corner. He approached them and asked, "What's going on here?" One of the boys looked up and replied, "Oh, we are just playing a little 'craps'." To which the teacher responded, "Oh, that's fine, I thought you were praying!"

As far out as this sounds, it reflects the tragedy that has happened in too many of our public schools-prayer is forbidden, but "crap shooting" and almost all manner of other evils are permitted.

Students are learning too much about sex in the classrooms and have started practicing it more and more before marriage. Birth control pills and other contraceptives are being used in increasing amounts. In spite of all these preventives, there are still more unwanted pregnancies and illegitimate births among high school girls than ever before!

Then in college, it is now common practice for boys and girls to share the same dormitory, the same apartment and the same bed.

There are few rules, curfews or restrictions.

In the last few years the "good girls" have become odd-balls and called prudes. Pre-marital sex is as much a college sport as football.

Drug peddling has become a problem of epidemic proportions in almost every school! Fist fights, knife and gun carrying and profane language are being used by pupils and teachers. Discipline problems prevail in staggering numbers. Young girls are being raped and immorality is practiced as the "in" thing!

No wonder many teachers are quitting. No wonder many students are graduating from high school and trying to enter college without even the level of an eighth grade education.

All of this disarray is the product of a school system that has for the most part turned its back on God! An education without moral and spiritual guidelines is extremely dangerous. Our kids have good intentions, but they must be channeled! Some may say, this is the responsibility of the churches! But I say, Christianity is a philosophy of life and is like breathing . . . it cannot be stopped at the school steps for the student or the teacher! This country's greatness is because of God and because we didn't let school yard boundaries stop our personal relationship with our God!

It seems the floodgates to all kinds of evil and permissiveness were opened wide when prayer and Bible reading were no longer permitted in the classroom and Christian teachers' voices were silenced! It is truly amazing just how many Christian kids have remained anchored through these years. The right road should be made easier for them, and we have a right and a responsibility to make it easier.

These godless thieves, disciples of Satan, have tried to steal the faith in God and His Word from the hearts of our youth! They have succeeded with far too many! It's time for the people of God to stand up and stop it! Together, we must recapture our lost freedoms!

Our past and our future demand it!

CHAPTER SIX

THE THIEVES STOLE OUR FAITH!

The birth of our country began with the fires of Freedom burning in the hearts of our founding fathers, with great emphasis on Freedom to worship. One of the first symbols was at the landing at Jamestown where a cross was planted, followed by the first Thanksgiving of the early pilgrims in Massachusetts. This was a time of expression of gratitude to God for our country and our freedom.

Today we continue to celebrate this holy day. It is stated in The American Heritage Dictionary of the English "Thanksgiving Day - a United States National Holiday set apart for giving thanks to God, celebrated on the fourth Thursday of November." Even the Supreme Court opens its sessions with the phrase "God save this honorable court" which began with our forefathers.

This is bewildering to some when our Supreme Court Sessions open with prayer calling on God to "Save the honorable Court" and on the other hand it is ruled unconstitutional if a school teacher opened her class with prayer.

Which brings up the question of when was the decision made concerning the Separation of Church and State. *Is* there a separation or is this a myth set forth as fact to those Americans that are uninformed concerning the Bill of Rights.

In an article in *Charisma*, November 1982, Dr. M.G. (Pat) Robertson, president of the Christian

Broadcasting Network and Chancellor of CBN University, explains his defense for the Prayer Amendment when he appeared before the United States Senate Judiciary Committee recently urging the committee's approval of Senate Joint Resolution 199, President Reagan's proposed Constitutional Amendment on school prayer.

The article states "Robertson told the committee:

"We often hear of the 'constitutionally mandated separation of church and state. Of course, as you know, that phrase appears nowhere in the Constitution or the Bill of Rights. It was in fact, a phrase used in a letter by Thomas Jefferson sent in 1802 to the Danbury Baptist Association, which had aroused his ire by criticism of one of his policies.''

Robertson explained that when Jefferson clarified his position three years later in his second inaugural address, there was no mention of "separation of church and state." Instead Jefferson used these words: "In matters of religion I have considered that its free exercise is placed by the Constitution independent of the power of the central government. I have therefore undertaken on no occasion to prescribe the the religious exercise suited to it (i.e. the central government) but have left them, as the Constitution found them, under the direction and discipline of the church or state authorities."

Robertson told the committee that this phrase is found in the constitution of another nation. It states, "The state shall be separate from the church, and the church from the school." Robertson continued, "Those words are not in the Constitution of the United States, but that of the Union of Soviet Socialist Republics - an atheistic nation sworn to the destruction of the United States of America . . ."

". . . To emphasize the enormity of the problem, Robertson reminded the committee of such decisions as the Supreme Court's refusal to overturn the ruling in the Nederland, New York, case "which denied the right of high school students to be accommodated for voluntary religious activities after school, even though all other student clubs were accommodated by the school."

Robertson also cited a federal court ruling in a Florida case (Chamberlin vs. Dade County Board) that the "showing of films depicting various religious happenings in the history of our nation were unconstitutional. In short, in Florida the students could not view the landing at Jamestown because a cross was planted there; the first Thanksgiving of the Pilgrims in Massachusetts because they thanked God; George Washington kneeling at prayer at Valley Forge; or the Virginia patriots at Bruton Parish Church."

The court rulings have brought confusion, according to Robertson. "The Supreme court opens its sessions with the phrase, 'God save this honorable court.' Yet that act would be unconstitutional if said by a school principal."

In his concluding remarks, Robertson said that, "the American people overwhelmingly want a reversal of the anti-religious court rulings of the past 20 years."

He added that his personal polls made from a sampling of people in 27,000 American communities indicated that 96 percent of those responding favored a constitutional amendment to restore religious liberties.

With our country in an era of so called "contemporary thinking," it is interesting that the majority of American people still favor a Constitutional Amendment restoring religious liberties. America is "one nation under God" because of the faith of our founding fathers.

As we examine the principals in which our nation was formed, it is important that we as Americans take another look at the faith, courage and character of the man who has been named "The Father of our Country!"

George Washington became the first president of our United States on April 30, 1789, in New York City. History records that the streets were jammed with thousands of people from far and wide who came to witness this historic occasion.

A great procession moved down Broad Street to Wall Street and to the Federal Building to where George Washington took the oath of office.

However, before this the church bells rang throughout the city and the people were called to the house of God and went upon their knees in prayer. They prayed that God would especially anoint, guide and direct this man who was becoming their first President.

Our nation was born and cradled in prayer by our founding fathers. The Secretary of the Senate, W.W. Livingston, gave the oath of office as thousands watched and listened breathlessly.

George Washington, just as all other Presidents who followed have done, swore to uphold the office of the President of the United States to protect, preserve and defend the Constitution of the United States.

However, it is said that as George Washington responded by saying, "I swear," he then did a very touching thing. He took the Bible from Secretary Livingston's hands and very reverently and respectfully pressed it to his lips and kissed it. Then he added, "So help me God." Every president sworn into office since that day has repeated that prayer . . . "So help me God!"

This gives us a deep look into the heart of the man who is called the "Father of our Country!"

One must admire his respect for the Bible that would cause him on another occasion to say, "It is impossible to govern our nation without God and His Word." Yes, he is rightfully called "The Father of our Country."

It was George Washington who coined the phrase, "For God and Country." It was he who was selected by his peers to be the Chairman of the Committee that drafted the Constitution of the United States.

Someone who made a study of George Washington's life said, "When you examine all of the stories about George Washington and then you read the historical accounts of George Washington by the men who knew him, you are led to believe that all of the stories and all of the legends still fall short of the sterling qualities and the character of this great man.''

Someone asked the question, ''What was the difference between George Washington and the other world leaders such as Alexander, Napoleon and Adolph Hitler?'' The response was this one, ''Other world leaders got to the top by trampling over people and by putting them down by force, power and bloodshed. But George Washington reached the top by ''reaching down'' to help and to assist others. He was a humble, modest man who truly loved God, his country and his fellowman.''

Some have the story that when one would walk as a visitor into the halls of Congress and would ask, ''Which man is George Washington?'' The response was, ''You will know George Washington when it comes time for prayer because he will be the only man on his knees.''

He was a recognized surveyor, agriculturist, soldier and statesman of world renown, but most of all he was known because he lived by his faith, his courage and his convictions!

I would not even suggest that George Washington's character was unblemished. There was only one truly good man who walked upon this earth . . . He is Jesus Christ. George Washington had his faults but he rose above them and became a Godly man who is respected and honored as no other American.

To better understand the roots of our heritage, notice three wonderful things about the Father of our country; his Christian character, his high moral standards and his strong reliance upon God.

HIS CHRISTIAN CHARACTER

George Washington's Christian character was demonstrated even when there were severe consequences involved. The little story that is told of him chopping down the cherry tree is but one small example. Though he realized there would be punishment to follow when he told this incident to his father, he still confessed it!

Once, I had the privilege of walking on the "Ferry Farm" (George Washington's boyhood home) located on the bands of the Rappahannock River at Fredericksburg, Virginia. No, I didn't see the stump where George Washington supposedly chopped down the cherry tree but I did see many of the old landmarks talked about in history.

I saw the original foundation of George Washington's boyhood home. I stood on the banks of the Rappahannock where it is believed that George Washington threw the stone (or perhaps the silver dollar) across that river. Many memories stirred my heart as I walked on what I considered to be "Holy Ground." My guide asked if I wanted to try and throw a silver dollar across the Rappahannock as George Washington did. I said "No, money just doesn't go as far these days!"

George Washington's Christian character is also exemplified in the story that is told when he was Commander in Chief of our Armies.

One day he sent a message to his officers in command that bluntly stated, "The blessings and protection of Heaven are at all times necessary but especially so in times of public distress and danger. The General hopes and trusts that every officer in command will endeavor to live and act as becomes a Christian soldier defending the dearest rights and liberties of his country.''

Can you imagine words like this coming from the pen and the heart of the Commander of Chief of our armies today? Oh, I pray to God this kind of command, this kind of direction would be given the officers in our armed forces. This is not to say that we don't have some genuine Christian leaders in our military services because we do. There are just too few of them!

Truly, we thank God for every Christian we have serving in public office. George Washington's strong Christian character caused him to beseech even his soldiers and officers to live, act and talk as Christian soldiers.

HIS HIGH MORAL STANDARDS

George Washington is also well known for his high moral standards. I am thinking especially of his convictions on the profane use of God's name.

He detested the use of profanity and so wrote this message to his soldiers and his officers and I quote, ''The General is sorry to be informed that the foolish and wicked practice of profane cursing and swearing - a vice heretofore little known in the American Army - is growing into fashion. He hopes that the officers will, by example as well as influence, endeavor to check it, and that both they and the men will reflect that we can have little hope of the blessing of Heaven on our arms if we insult it by our impiety and folly.

Added to this, it is a vice so mean and low, without any temptation that every man of sense and character detests and despises it.''

Can you imagine a message like this being published today?

This communique went to his officers in his armed forces imploring them to discontinue the taking of God's name in vain, declaring that we could not take God's hallowed name in vain and expect our God to bless and stand by us!!

It is obvious George Washington was a man of high moral standards, and strong Christian character. If only today we could realize how desperately this quality is still needed in our land as never before!

We cannot expect to take the name of our God in vain, today, and also expect to be the beneficiaries of the blessings of Heaven! I pray the Lord will convict the American people of this sin from the "Church House" to the "White House!" May we humbly return to the faith of the Father of our Country!

HIS STRONG RELIANCE UPON GOD

George Washington demonstrated a strong reliance upon God. He is known as a man of prayer. The occasion that is remembered most in my mind is when George Washington went down on his knees in the thickets in the deep snow at Valley Forge.

At that dark hour his soldiers were discouraged . . . many had worn out their shoes . . . some had only rags for uniforms . . . they were all cold, freezing and thousands were dying! It is reported that some only had "hogheads" for shoes for their bleeding, frostbitten feet!

It was said George Washington's army could be traced by blood stains upon the snow from the bleeding feet of his soldiers! It looked impossible for that handful of men to make that Declaration of Independence stick under such seemingly impossible odds.

But at that dark hour George Washington fell upon his knees and sought the face of God in prayer! I am sure the angels must have wept as he prayed for the help, the courage and wisdom of our Creator who determines the destinies of men and nations. God answered that prayer and I believe this was the turning point in the Revolutionary War! In my humble opinion America is more personified at Valley Forge than at any other place in our history when George Washington went to his knees in intercessory prayer to God!

In George Washington's farewell address to the people of the United States on September 18, 1796 he substantiates the importance of religious principal when he said, "Of all the dispositions and habits which lead to political prosperity, religion and morality are indispensable supports. In vain would that man claim the tribute of patriotism who should labor to subvert these great pillars of human happiness - these firmest props of the duties of men and citizens. The mere politician, equally with the pious man, ought to respect and to cherish them. A volume could not trace all their connections with private and public felicity. Let this simply be asked, (where is the security for property, for reputation, for life, if the sense of religious obligation desert the oaths which are the instruments of investigation in courts of justice?) And let us with caution indulge the supposition that morality can be maintained without religion. Whatever may be conceded to the influence of refined education on minds of peculiar structure, reason and structure both forbid us to expect that national morality can prevail in exclusion of religious principle . . .''

He continues to say "observe good faith and justice toward all nations. Cultivate peace and harmony with all. Religion and morality enjoin this conduct.''

The faith of the Father of our country must be kept alive in our hearts and in our country today if we expect to continue to live in "one nation under God!''

Make no mistake about it - America was born on her knees in submission to Almighty God with a Bible in her hands and I'm convinced the only way we can get our country on its feet again in this crisis hour is to get our nation on its knees again!

Article 1 of the Bill of Rights reads, "Congress shall make no law respecting an establishment of religion, or prohibiting the free exercise thereof''

This article explicitly states that no laws are to be made that "prohibit the free (or voluntary) exercises of religion.'' This means anywhere by anybody!

It is obvious from Article 1 of the Bill of Rights that the Supreme Court is overstepping the boundaries of their authority to stop praying in our public schools since no laws can be made that would "prohibit the free (voluntary) exercise of religion'' in this country.

Our high court must be reminded again and again that their task is to interpret the laws not make new ones!

Cecil Todd discusses with President Gerald Ford at the White House, during his tenure of office, some of the spiritual needs of our nation.

At a recent briefing at the White House, Cecil Todd and several religious leaders from across the nation meet with President Reagan. In the background you can see Jimmy Swaggart, Adrian Rogers and Tim LaHaye.

CHAPTER SEVEN

THE THIEVES STOLE PRAYER FROM OUR PUBLIC SCHOOLS!

God's message to America, I believe is found in the following words:

> "If my people; which are called by my name will humble themselves and pray, and seek my face, and turn from their wicked ways, then will I hear from heaven, and will forgive their sin, and heal their land." II Chronicles 7:14

Many have asked if it is possible to get prayer back in our public schools. After 20 years, can the tide be turned?

I believe with all my heart that we can see our children's stolen freedom of prayer restored. But it will take a united effort from Christians all across America.

The effort, however, must start on an individual level. We must all do what we can!

To see this end result, each of us must:

Pray - Matthew 18:19 says, ". . . if two of you shall agree as touching anything that they shall ask, it shall be done of them of my Father which is in heaven." The power of prayer cannot and must not be tossed aside lightly, especially in a battle such as this that is without a doubt, "spiritual warfare."

Prayer is still our greatest weapon. Prayer will move more than just mountains, prayer will move God and with God, all things are possible. I believe God wants prayer back into our schools more than all of us put together.

I have seen the power of prayer melt hearts and change the attitude of people in positions of influence and authority, and we need that now more than ever.

Remember Daniel, the great prophet of old, was thrown into a den of lions because he dared to disobey the king by praying to God. But God stopped the mouths of the lions and delivered Daniel not only "in" the lions den, but also "from" the lions in the den.

Daniel's God is still alive and well and ready to help us win the battles for right today.

Let's bathe our efforts in fervent prayer. The Bible says that "The fervent prayer of a righteous man availeth much." (James 5:16)

So much is at stake in our schools and in our nations. If we continue to allow the devil's disciples to kick God out of His rightful place in our country, I fear the consequences! "Be not deceived, God is not mocked!" (Gal. 6:7)

The heart cries of the multitudes must be heard! Abraham Lincoln said in his famous Gettysburg Address that we must . . . "have government of the people, by the people and for the people . . ."

We are the people, the majority of Americans who love the Lord. Let's pray and humble ourselves before the Lord so He can heal our land.

GET INFORMED - It is my prayer that in reading this book that you will develop a burden for our nation and our rights, such as prayer in our public schools, that have been stolen by Satan's thieves from our school kids!

Also, get informed at election time. Know which men and women are godly and want to recapture our many stolen freedoms!

Study the voting records of those in office and make sure their convictions are dictating how they vote. Don't listen to what they say in a heated election campaign! Some politicians will say almost anything to get elected! Examine their past voting records!

GET VOCAL - Madalyn Murray O'Hair removed prayer from the public schools by simply getting noisy. She let her voice be heard, starting with a letter to the editor of the local paper. To express your views, don't be timid about:

1. Writing letters - write your senators and representatives, both national and on the state level. Let them know your feelings and how you expect them to follow through on these issues.

While you are at it, write letters to your local school officials, principal, superintendant and school board members. You'll be amazed and encouraged by how much input your handwritten letter will have on these people in authority.

2. Write letters to the editors - most newspapers have a policy where they will print a different letter from any reader once a month. This is a great way

to inform people, and inspire others to get on the front lines for God! This does not cost a thing, yet is a great way to minister to others, plus express yourself.

3.   Tell others - Sunday Schools, sewing circles, businessmen, any group can make an impact. By informing others, and expressing yourself to the public through petitions and letter writing campaigns, you can see results.

4. Be a Part - There are ministries spending millions of dollars a year to defend our Christian rights. Revival Fires is on the forefront, and has been for almost twenty years, trying to do our part to inform and inspire Americans to action before it's too late.

We, as Christians, deserve what we are getting and it will get even worse unless we get involved, and do something to stop it!

The spiritual climate is ripe for revival in this country and for the recovery of many of our stolen freedoms that have been lost in recent years because of the Devil's thieves!

But it will take a united move and involvement of the people of God all across our land to accomplish it - but win, we can. With God all things are still possible!

Our investment is too high in our public schools to forsake them. I believe Christian schools are great and I support them and am grateful for the morals, quality education and spiritual background they give thousands of students.

But, relying on them totally is unwise! They are

great for those who can afford it, but what about those who cannot? Godly lessons must be taught to every child in America, including in our public schools, but not just in Christian schools.

Plus, we are paying taxes every year into our public schools regardless of whether your child attends private or public schools. You are paying double!

We must save our "investment."

We must go recapture our freedoms, stolen by the Devil's thieves!

And, the time to start is now!

CHAPTER EIGHT

OUR PRESIDENT JOINS THE FIGHT!

Following is an interview on the President's proposed voluntary school prayer amendment:

Question: Will the amendment overrule, abolish or modify the First Amendment to the constitution?

President Reagan: No. The voluntary school prayer amendment will be consistent with the original purpose of the First Amendment, which was to enhance the opportunities of citizens to worship as they see fit. For 170 years after the adoption of the First Amendment, prayer was permitted in the public schools. In 1962, the Supreme Court held that prayer in the public schools violated the First Amendment provision forbidding and "establishment of religion.

Justice Potter Stewart, in a strong dissent from the Court's opinion, pointed out that the purpose of the Establishment Clause was to prevent the Federal Government from establishing an official religion. Justice Stewart pointed out that permitting school children to participate voluntarily in prayer is a far cry from designating a particular religion to which citizens must subscribe. He pointed out that the two Houses of Congress open their daily sessions with prayer, that our coins, our Pledge of Allegiance and our National Anthem all reflect the truth that "we are a religious people whose institutions presuppose a Supreme Being." Engel V. Vitale, 370 U.S. 421 (1962) (Stewart, J. dissenting).

Question: How will the amendment guarantee that nobody will be coerced into participating in prayer or religious exercise?

Reagan: The amendment will guarantee that no person shall be required by the United States or by any state to participate in prayer. Lower federal court decisions have suggested, for instance, that prayers by unofficial groups of students who congregate after class hours of their own volition are not really voluntary because other students might feel subtle pressure to join in the prayer. The amendment will reject such an approach.

Question: What is to prevent school districts from imposing particular religious doctrines on school children?

Reagan: The amendment will rely on two factors to guard against the imposition of sectarian beliefs:

First, the American political tradition is one of respect for diversity and for freedom of religious expression. It would be wrong to assume that states and localities would seek to stifle diversity or to offend members of their communities who hold minority religious views. In fact, prior to 1962, local school authorities demonstrated a respect both for religion and diverse views about religion.

Second, the amendment will absolutely forbid public schools or other government agencies from requiring anyone to participate in any prayer of religious exercise. Anyone who is offended by the content of any prayer - whether he is a member of a minority religious group, an atheist or anyone else - can simply refuse to participate; this constitutional right of refusal will be an absolute safeguard against the imposition of narrow sectarian dogmas on school children. Indeed, any reference to a "personal" God who is more than a mere "life-force" might be "denominational" in so far as it reflected the general beliefs of Judaism and Christianity to the exclusion of those who reject the idea of a personal God.

Question: Will the amendment affect other public institutions besides public schools?

Reagan: Yes, but this provision would effect little or no change in present judicial interpretations of the First Amendment. As Justice Stewart pointed out in his dissent in Engle V. Vitale, prayer is an important part of our national heritage and of our daily community life. Prayer in public places other than schools - in public parks, in prisons, in hospitals, in legislatures, in Presidential Inaugural Addresses - has never been held to violate the constitution. The United States Supreme Court begins all its sessions with reference to Almighty God. The amendment would reaffirm this interpretation, subject to the right of every individual to refuse to participate in prayer or religious exercise.

Question: Would the amendment have any intended effect on pending court actions against prayers in sessions of Congress and against the retention of chaplains in the armed services?

Reagan: The amendment would reaffirm the constitutionality of prayers in congress and of armed service chaplains.

Another thing I urge people to do is to be a friend to the school officials and share the Lord with them. Minister in love to the teachers and the principals.

Too often we Christians get so caught up in our zeal to be even polite, we fail to speak up for our convictions. Yet we must show love in our actions and words to lead others to the Lord.

Another real ministry in the schools is our own children.

As parents, you have the opportunity to carry that youngster to church and to pray with him at home.

Your child can be the "salt" (the flavor!) for a school of hungry students. Help him or her understand how to win others to Jesus as soon as they are old enough and mature enough in the Lord.

Most public schools will no longer allow ministers or evangelists in to talk to the kids about Jesus Christ. Our Christian kids must be the missionaries to our public schools! Some have even said, "the public schools in America have become the number one mission field in the world!"

There are many ways to evangelize our students - we must use them - or lose them!

This historic occasion happened on the sidewalk in front of the White House . . . Cecil Todd witnesses to America's number 1 atheist, Madalyn Murray O'Hair and offers her a Bible. She refused the Bible, but when her followers were offered Bibles, they all took them! Praise God!

CHAPTER NINE

RECAPTURING THE GOODS FROM THE THIEVES!

Though having voluntary prayer back in the public schools is a driving, important goal, yet our steps to point our public schools to Christian ideals should be much stronger than that.

As this book goes to press, Revival Fires is in the process of distributing 50,000 more Bibles to school kids without one.

We've designed special folders that children are excited about in school. It has the picture of Jackson Bailey's "creation" on one side and the Lord's Prayer on the other. We have distributed over 400,000 of these.

One teacher asked me for 50 folders for her class. Later, she told me she held one of them up before her class and explained to them how God made us and that we needed prayer in our schools.

One of the students shyly raised his hand and asked, "Teacher, where did you get those folders? We haven't seen anything like them around here."

The teacher explained where she got it and then said, "and, I just happen to have forty-nine more - but you know the Supreme Court decision has said that I cannot give these to you because they have scriptures, prayer and God's name on them, so I don't know what to do . . . ''

All of a sudden the class came alive discussing this issue and trying to come up with a solution.

Finally one of the kids came up with a bright idea:

"Teacher, if it is wrong for you to give them away, why don't you just put them on a chair out in the hall, turn your head, and we will steal them and go repent later!"

Isn't that something?

Only a kid could think of something like that. But you know, that class did more than that, they took every folder she had, and some of them even emptied their pockets of their lunch money so she could get more! The whole school got folders as a result of that incident.

Our children are hungry for the Word of God and it is our responsibility to get it to them. Nothing is more exciting than to see young people on fire for God.

The Bible says to "be as wise as serpents and as gentle as doves." I believe that holds a key for us today.

These folders are one creative way to get God's Word in the schools.

Can you think of other ways?

If you are a Christian teacher in a public school, you have a great opportunity.

Why not try practicing voluntary prayer in your classroom?

Just begin by opening your class with prayer. inform your students that their participation is voluntary. Invite them to meditate and pray.

Others who have started this have been amazed and pleased at the favorable response, plus the overall attitude of their class seems to change.

If you are challenged by any of the parents, school officials or anyone else, just inform them of your right in Article 1 of the Bill of Rights that states, "Congress shall make no law respecting an establishment of religion, *or prohibiting the free exercise thereof...*"

Across the years, we all have learned that rights we do not use, we soon lose! Too often only the rights of the minorities are considered. This isn't right. We are a government of the people, by the people and for the people!

Also, with enough support from Christian parents, many public school officials are now teaching a course in Bible literature as a part of their school curriculum. The response by the students has been very encouraging. Many school officials recognize the strong literary value of the Bible, but also realize that through this method, they are able to teach God's Word without any violation of the widespread interpretation of the Supreme Court's decision.

Some teachers are using the book, *The Peaceable Kingdom* as their textbook. My personal examination of this book revealed it was basically all Scripture with comments that related only to the literary value of the Scripture. The book is co-edited by Alvin Lee, Hope Lee, W.T. Jewkes and Northrup Frye and is published by Harcourt Brace Jovanovich, Inc. in New York.

While this approach may not meet our highest desires, it still is an improvement over what most public schools are doing, and I believe is an example of what other schools can do if it is brought to their attention and are encouraged to do so.

If the public schools in your community, city or area are not already offering a similar course, suggest some rewarding course, the encouragement of you and your friends to the school board and officials could get things moving in that direction. One of my mottos across the years has been, "It's better to have tried and failed than to have never tried!"

Tragic but true, it is easier to get into Africa to preach Jesus Christ today than it is to get into most public schools in America! God help us! Since most schools have closed their doors to Christianity, it is most important that born again teachers, students and school officials realize they are like missionaries to our public schools.

The Royalheirs, Cecil Todd and Pastor Larry Ansel pose for photos just ahead of taping a one-hour TV special in Larry's church, the "Camp Meeting Church of the Rockies" in Denver, Colorado.

CHAPTER TEN

THE ROLE OF REVIVAL FIRES!

Sometime ago, I began gathering one million prayer petitions to take to President Reagan. It took two years to fulfill this assignment God had given to me.

These one million prayer petitions came from all fifty states, and filled fifty mail bags, weighing over 1,200 lbs. More than $250,000 was spent in this effort! It was worth every dollar of it, because of how God used that one million petitions.

When I delivered them to the White House, I was told by the mail officials there that it was the largest number of petitions ever delivered to the White House for any issue of public concern.

I've gathered some news clippings of that event and the results.

I'm enclosing them in this book to show just how God can use us, if we will let Him!

EVANGELIST CECIL TODD DELIVERS PRAYER PETITIONS
By Paul Keegan
Ottaway News Service
WASHINGTON - These are the facts, according to Dr. Cecil Todd, the television evangelist from Joplin, Mo:

"Since prayer was taken out of our public schools (by a Supreme Court decision) on June 17, 1963:

- "Crime has increased at an unprecedented 300 percent;
- "One million teen-age school girls are getting pregnant each year;
- "Four hundred thousands are having their babies aborted (murdered);
- "Hundreds of school age young people committed suicide last year;
- "Eighty percent of our school kids are on drugs;
- "Drinking, smoking, vandalism and discipline have become a mojor problem."

Since the Supreme Court decision sparked this moral decline in America almost 19 years ago Todd reasons, a massive nationwide campaign to reinstate school prayer would halt the decline and put America back on the path of spiritual revival.

Toward that end, Todd, director of Revival Fires Ministries" and a nationally syndicated TV preacher, held a colorful press conference Thursday morning to announce the delivery of one million signatures to the White House urging the president and Congress "to return this treasured freedom of voluntary prayer back into our public schools."

Todd is not advocating the forced recitation of a Christian prayer, though he has suggested "The Lord's Prayer" for schools as the most non-sectarian, beautiful prayer of all.

Rather, his movement, which he says has 400 organizations behind it, urges the setting aside of a certain portion of each day to allow students to pray or meditate together or separately in whatever way they wish.

Todd said he is not pushing for any particular piece of legislation to institute prayer time in schools.

Todd said he hoped to meet with President Reagan, who he said supports voluntary school prayer. Todd did not agree with critics who complain that Reagan has not done enough on school prayer, but he said he thought one year should be enough time for Congress and the President to take some action.

"I'm convinced the turmoil in our country and the trouble in our public schools can be traced to our allegiance - or our non-allegiance - to Almighty God!" Todd told the press gathering.

"I believe America's real problems are not financial but spiritual; history will verify that the further we get away from God, the more problems we will have. I believe there is a connection between prayer and Bible reading taken out of our public schools and the godless slide America is experiencing; if our founding fathers intended to stop prayers in our public schools, they would have done so two hundred years ago."

"I'm not saying that Jesus Christ be put in the schools as the state-sponsored religion," said William Murray, also a speaker at the press conference. "If they want to meet each morning to practice their religious beliefs, they should be allowed to use public property in this manner."

Murray, the son of atheist activist Madalyn Murray O'Hair, converted to Christianity two years ago and is active in the school prayer movement.

When asked why students could not just pray silently, Murray said students should be free to form prayer groups. He quoted Matthew chapter 18, verse 20; "For where two or three are gathered together in my name, there am I in the midst of them."

This led to a post-press conference question to Todd on where the limits on religious activity would be drawn. It was suggested to him that tax-paying parents may not approve of public schools being used for demon worship.

"That needs to be in the hands of school officials to determine the limits by which this (religion freedom) can be exercised," he said. "I see particular danger in cults and voodo expounded by groups not compatible with the beliefs of a majority of Americans."

The press conference looked something like the set of a television show, with a hugh red, white and blue banner behind the pulpit proclaiming that Todd and his entourage were "White House Bound."

Fifty mail sacks containing the signatures were dumped in front of the preacher, as were dozens of blue paperback Bibles, neatly lined up. The book, "From God With Love," is a paraphrase of the New Testament printed by Revival Fires and distrubuted to school children.

The press was provided with a full-color brochure with a painting of God creating heaven and earth on the cover and biographical information on Todd inside.

A resident of Joplin since 1964, Todd was one of eleven children and grew up in the Kiamachi Mountains in southeastern Oklahoma. He was "converted to Christ" at age 15 in a one room school house in the mountains of Southeastern Oklahoma and started preaching at age 18, the biography says.

Eighteen years ago, he founded the Joplin-based Christian Evangelizers Association, Inc., or "Revival Fires." His "Revival Fires" TV show has been aired since 1965, making it the third longest running TV religious program ever, 850 half-hour shows and six one-specials have been produced.

At the same time, the local Joplin, MO paper, "The Globe" reported:

CECIL TODD, PETITIONS ON WAY TO WASHINGTON
By Kit Brothers
Staff Writer

Clutching a Bible and a "creation" folder, Cecil Todd, president of Revival Fires, Inc., proclaimed that he was beginning a "mission ordained by God" Wednesday afternoon before he left for Washington D.C. with his petitions to restore what he contends has been prohibited . . . prayer in public schools.

Todd held a press conference at the Joplin Municipal Airport just before boarding a private jet. He will deliver what he says, "Are one million signatures" to the White House at 2:30 p.m. today.

Morton C. Blackwell, special assistant to the president, will receive the "Prayer petitions," which will be placed in the White House archives, Todd said.

The Joplin evangelist, who is battling the 1963 U.S. Supreme Court ruling that banned mandatory prayer in public schools, said he might meet also with President Ronald Reagan.

Standing in front of a banner reading "White House Bound" and in front of some of the 50 petition bearing mail bags, Todd said his trip coincides with a convention of atheists led by Madalyn Murray O'Hair, whose suits resulted in the 1963 court ruling.

Her son, Bill Murray, is Todd's co-worker in supporting prayer in school. The two men will lead a three-day vigil, praying for the atheists' salvation, Todd said.

Todd also will hold a press conference at 10 a.m. today at the Washington Marriott Hotel. Religious leaders and members of Congress will attend, he said.

Fifty school children will carry the 50 mail bags to the White House to emphasize the children's concern, Todd said. School officials have carried the issue far beyond the court's original intention, he said, citing examples of schools holding no Christmas nativity pageants and of calling Easter Vacation "spring breaks."

"Why don't the atheists go out and start their own private schools?" he said. "Their job is tearing down, not building up . . ."

"God has been the glue that has held this country together."

In the past few months, Revival Fires has distributed to children 10,000 Bibles and 250,000 folders depicting divine creation and the Lord's Prayer.

Todd spent two years collecting the signatures, which he planned to deliver during President Jimmy Carter's administration. However, he said Carter might have used the issue as political fuel, since that delivery was scheduled during the last presidential campaign.

"I didn't want it used as a political football."

At the close of the Wednesday press

conference, Todd led a prayer, interrupted only by the crying of his infant grand-daughter, Charity Gail.

Several other children, elementary through high-school helped Todd load the mail bags tied with red, white and blue ribbons, into the aircraft.

"Good luck," said grinning Chris Cook, 10, "but I guess since you have the Lord with you, you don't need 'luck' do you?"

What happened after I presented those petitions to the White House was one of the most thrilling events of my life.

For the first time in 20 years, an American President had the courage to go on national television and announce his support of returning voluntary prayer to the public schools.

Read the local Joplin paper's account of this great event;

JOPLIN EVANGELIST SAYS PETITIONS TRIGGERED REAGAN ANNOUNCE-MENT
By Wally Kennedy
Staff Writer

Upon returning Thursday night from his Rose Garden meeting with President Ronald Reagan, Joplin evangelist Cecil Todd said he was "overwhelmed" by the president's decision to "use the power of his position to restore voluntary prayer in the public schools."

In a brief press conference at the Joplin Municipal Airport, Todd said, "Our campaign for a constitutional amendment has jarred loose the political structure in Washington. I am extremely encouraged."

While his wife clutched a Bible autographed by the President and Nancy Reagan, he said, "There is no doubt that the delivery of the one million petitions triggered the president's announcement today.

"The petitions indicated to the President that he has a broad base of support from all 50 states. The President can now move with confidence."

On April 9, Todd delivered a million petitions to the White House. The petitions requested that the President use his office to push for a constitutional amendment on prayer in public schools and institutions.

Todd, who said the President complimented him for the delivery of the petitions, cited an article on the most recent issue of Newsweek Magazine to back his claim that the petitions triggered the President's announcement Thursday.

The article, in part, said: ". . . the postal pro-prayer crusade has persuaded some Reagan men that the measure has broad-based support and is therefore safe to take a stand on."

He said the president seeks a return to the situation before 1962 when voluntary prayer was not thought to conflict with the First Amendment.

In 1963, the U.S. Supreme Court banned mandatory prayer in public schools.

The proposed amendment, which will be drafted "in the most acceptable language" by the Department of Justice by the end of the next week, will provide two simple guarantees, he said. They are:

- The federal government and the Constitution will not prohibit individual or group prayer in public schools or other public institutions.
- The right of those who choose not to participate in school prayer will be guaranteed and no one will be required to participate.

Approximately 125 religious leaders participated in the Rose Garden meeting.

The following was published in *Newsweek,* on May 10, 1982.

PRAYER-MAIL CRUSADE CONVERTS REAGAN

"Proponents of a constitutional amendment to allow prayer in public schools have deluged the White House with one-million letters and postcards last month The faithful showed so much political devotion that their prayers may be answered. Amendment backers now expect President Reagan to reiterate his support for the bill this week. In general, Reagan's aides have urged him to soft pedal his views on "Social Issue" amendment proposals to avoid unnecessary controversies. But the postal pro-prayer crusade has persuaded some Reagan men that the measure has broad-based support and is therefore safe to take a strong stand on."

And the Associated Press reported from Washington D.C.:

Washington (AP) - President Reagan, declaring he wants to "restore a freedom our Constitution was always meant to protect," called Thursday for an amendment to allow voluntary group prayer in public schools.

"No one must ever be forced or coerced or pressured to take part in any religious exercise, but neither should the government forbid religious practice," the President told a gathering of religious leaders during a ceremony in the Rose Garden.

"The amendment we'll propose will restore the right to pray."

Reagan did not say precisely what language he believed such an amendment should contain, but in the name of freedom, have taken a freedom away. "For the sake of religious tolerance they have forbidden religious practice in our public classroom," he said.

"No one will ever convince me that

a moment of voluntary prayer will harm a child or threaten a school or state. But I think it can strengthen our faith in a Creator who alone has the power to bless America," he added.

Referring to the 1962 Supreme Court ruling that declared school prayer unconstitutional under the First Amendment, Reagan said:

"I have never believed that the oft-quoted amendment was supposed to protect us from religion. It was to protect religion from government tyranny."

"Together, let us take up the challenge to reawaken America's religious and moral heart, recognizing the deep and abiding faith in God." He said a specific proposal would be submitted to Congress soon.

"Changing the constitution is a mammouth task," said Reagan, speaking from a podium under a hot sun. "It should never be easy, but in this case I believe we can restore a freedom that our Constitution was always meant to protect."

"Yet in recent years, well-meaning Americans have removed the rock upon which this great nation was founded."

"Experience teaches us that efforts to introduce religious practices into public schools generate the very inter-religious tension and conflict that the First Amendment was designed to prevent."

Other organizations signing the statement were the Baptist Joint Committee on Public Affairs, the National Coalition for Public Education and Religious Liberty, the National Jewish Community Relations Advisory Council and the Synagogue Council of America.

The Joplin paper further reported:

EVANGELIST TODD BELIEVES MISSION WITH PRAYER PETITIONS EFFECTIVE.

White House officials are considering 50 resolutions on the issue of prayer in public schools, according to Cecil Todd, President of Revival Fires Inc., Joplin, who last week took to Washington, D.C., petitions protesting the Supreme Court's ban on mandatory prayer.

Todd delivered a record million "prayer petitions" to Morton C. Blackwell, special assistant to President Ronald Reagan.

He was told that this was "the largest mandate from the American people calling for return of prayer to public schools" and that the petitions will have a strong influence in getting legislative action, Todd said.

In an interview Tuesday, Todd said Congress might pass a resolution on voluntary prayer, avoiding court action or constitutional amendment.

"There seems to be a point of confusion on whether the court over-rules voluntary prayer or mandatory prayer," Todd said. "If voluntary prayer has not been stopped, then I would like to know this . . ."

"Right now, in the minds of most school officials, they (students) don't have the right to pray . . . They only have the freedom not to pray, which isn't a freedom at all. It's a limitation . . ."

"Not that I want to see coerced prayer or some kind of state-written prayer."

Todd said, "they are trying at the White House level to lift the cloud of confusion on whether voluntary prayer was over-ruled."

Todd said he expects to meet with Reagan, who was not in Washington during the Easter weekend visit, in the next few weeks.

While in Washington, Todd said he offered a Bible to Madalyn Murray O'Hair, who was conducting an atheists' convention. The suits of Ms. O'Hair, who refused the Bible, resulted in the 1963 Supreme Court ruling. However, many of her atheist followers who were offered Bibles . . . took them!

If only we could have got to Madalyn Murray O'Hair when she was a tender hearted ten year old girl with God's Word and Jesus Christ, I don't believe we would be in the mess we are in today on this emotional issue! How many more potential Madalyn Murray O'Hairs do we have all around us today?

This 1000 foot long Prayer Petition is the longest petition (longer than three football fields) ever delivered to our nation's capitol in our 208 year history. Cecil Todd delivers one to Tip O'Neill and Howard Baker in late 1983 with the names of 100,000 who want voluntary prayer returned to our public schools.

One of the many packed auditoriums who were attracted to a Revival Fires crusade rally with Cecil Todd.

Dr. Cecil Todd visits with President Ronald Reagan during the taping of a segment for the Revival Fires TV program. Cecil Todd has been a Prayer Partner with President Reagan for many years.

CHAPTER ELEVEN

RECRUITING AN ARMY TO RECAPTURE OUR STOLEN GOODS!

As we see the shocking reality of the condition of our country today, we stand embarrassed and frustrated when we realize that the status of our nation is formed by "We the people" of our nation. The direction of our country is our responsibility! Our Lord said, "Occupy till I come!" We have allowed the devil's disciples to come in "while we played" and stole our goods!

It is unfortunate that for the past three or four decades moral, law abiding, God-fearing Americans have increasingly absorbed ourselves with our own little worlds.

We have spent our time with our families, our homes, our immediate communities and church activities. We have done too much playing and not enough praying (interceding!), too much feasting and not enough fasting! Our upper rooms have been turned into supper rooms!

By so doing, we have allowed no time for involvement concerning our nation. We have generally shunned modern politics and politicians.

Conservative citizens by the millions sought to detach themselves from the deterioration of their community and cities at large. The result has been an overwhelming number of basically law abiding citizens leaving the running of our communities and nation up to godless, worldly minded unregenerated people who want to be a "god unto themselves!"

It is in God's plan for us to be concerned with our families, church and communities, but His plan also includes the government of our cities and our nation.

Our neglect has sent our nation sliding toward national suicide.

Because of our selfish, self-centered and sinful ways we have been plunged into unprecedented violence, crime and immorality throughout the nation. Drugs, ilicit sex and humanistic philosophies have infiltered our neighborhood schools, poisoning and polluting the minds of our precious school kids.

We have the freedom to meet together as children of God, to praise Him and pray to Him because we live in a free country. If we lose our freedom as a nation, we lose our freedom to love and worship Him as we desire to!

Because we played too much and prayed too little, we, who are supposed to be the "salt" and the "light" did very little about the problems attacking and destroying the Christian foundations in our communities.

Some argue, these spiritual values must be learned in our homes and in our churches. I agree, but not just in our homes and churches. Christianity is a philosophy of life and must not be stopped by government owned property by public schools or seats of government, by students, teachers or legislators.

As Christians, Christ and His teachings go where we go! Our national motto is "One Nation Under God" and the Supreme Court of the 1950's declared "America is a Christian Nation!"

We must not make a mockery of our God or of the faith of our founding fathers by denying ourselves or our children the legacy we enjoy as Americans!

Our first responsibliity is to get this nation back to God. II Chronicles 7:14 says, "If my people, who are called by my name, will humble themselves and pray and seek my face and turn from their wicked ways, *then* will I hear from heaven and will forgive their sin and heal their land."

It happened many years ago at a crisis hour. The delegates of the First Continental Congress were assembled when word was received that Boston was under severe attack. The chaplain of Congress rose to his feet and read this verse, "Plead my cause, Oh Lord, with them that strive with me. Fight against them that fight against me. Take hold of shield and buckler and stand up for mine help." (Psalms 91:4)

After these words were read, all of the delegates and Congressmen stood with bowed heads and tears in their eyes as they prayed a prayer of repentance.

All of them stood with bowed heads but one, he was on his knees. That man was George Washington.

Almost every time Congress prayed, George Washington knelt in prayer. This must happen again to all America! The whole country needs to be brought to her knees in repentance. Prayer is still our most powerful weapon! We must pray more and play less!

The future of our nation may well be in the hands of our youth of today. God said, "Train up a child in the way he is to go and he will not depart from it." (Prov. 22:6) "The father of the righteous will greatly rejoice and he who begets a wise son will be glad in him." (Prov. 23:24 NASB)

After much serious thought on the matter, I'm convinced we need chaplains in our public schools and colleges!

After all, we recognized the value of chaplains in our House and Senate . . . in our prisons . . . and in all four branches of the Armed Services.

Why not in our public schools and in our colleges?

Every day our youth are faced with the illicit use of dope and drugs, drinking and drunkeness, immorality, profanity, illegitimate babies and abortions. The Devil is having a holiday in our schools. These kids need all the help they can get. They need someone they can not only talk to but also to pray to! Our school counselors have been given too little training and too many restrictions!

Qualified Chaplains in our schools could be the beginning of a new and better day for our young people!

Our country is not beyond hope. We the people, with the help of Almighty God, can and must offer solutions for the problems facing our communities, our schools, our cities and our nation. We can enjoy victories in our cities and over our great land if we will be the "salt" and the "light" for our communities as our Lord told us to do!!!

We must speak up and speak out for God, our

families and our country. It's time to get off our seats, onto our feet and into the streets with the saving message of Jesus Christ.

God is not America's last hope, God is America's only hope! The power behind us is greater than the task before us!

Yes, while we played, the thieves stole our goods! Now it's time for us to go forth and recapture our stolen freedoms!

Several times I have made reference to George Washington because he was our first president and is recognized as the "Father of our Country!"

I'm convinced that when he was on his knees before God, more than any other time, he was America personified! This country was born on it's knees with a Bible in it's hands. To get America on her feet again, we must once again get America on its knees again!

When Jesus rose from the dead he hit the devil in the head! In His powerful Name we must go forth and do the same, again and again.

"Thanks be unto God who gives us the victory through our Lord Jesus Christ!" (I Cor. 15:57)

CHAPTER TWELVE

THE ABORTION ABOMINATION

Four thousand unborn babies are murdered every day in America! That's one baby killed every twenty-one seconds and a staggering sixteen million murdered since the historic High Court decision on January 22, 1973.

The Supreme Court calls it "Abortion" — as do the doctors and the nurses — the politicians and even many of us. But God calls it "MURDER!" Multitudes of medical doctors have testified that the little unborn baby is alive in it's mother's womb!

By the time it is four weeks old, it is breathing — it has lungs! It's heart is beating and it is growing hair and fingernails! That precious unborn baby is alive! Every doctor in the world, "worth their salt", will tell you that baby is alive in it's mother's womb!

"It feels pain, too," according to Dr. Vincent J. Collins, Medical Professor at Northwestern University. Dr. Collins is co-author of a paper entitled, *"Fetal Pain And Abortion: The Medical Evidence!"*

It was from these medical findings that caused President Reagan to declare in one of his many pro-life speeches, "The unborn feel pain that is long and agonizing when an abortion is performed!"

The records show that in many major cities across our land, more precious little ones are aborted (killed) before they are born than babies that are born! Literally, hundreds of schools across our nation are closing or consolidating because of the sharp decline in babies being born.

These sixteen million unborn babies who have been killed since the High Court decision is now having a dramatic impact on our schools, colleges, churches, and yes, on our playgrounds too!

The most dangerous place in the world today is not in the shark-infested waters of the high seas or on the front lines of battle in a war or even in your car on New Year's Eve, but the most dangerous place on earth today is a baby in it's mother's womb! The chances of a little baby being killed (aborted!) while in it's mother's womb is higher than fifty percent!

What God intended as the safest of all places, the mother's womb, has now become the most dangerous! God help us!

No one is safe in a nation who will allow (and even underwrite the costs in many states!) it's defenseless little ones to be murdered before they can be born! Who do you think will be next? I can tell you — it's our Senior Citizens! Already the governor of Colorado has said on national television, "You elderly people need to die and get out of the way — make room for the younger people!"

These kinds of words make me fighting mad! If anyone needs to "get out of the way", it's that governor as far as I'm concerned! I'm persuaded our Senior Citizens are the backbone of America — the cream of our country! They have more real love in their hearts, praying-power and genuine compassion than all the rest of us put together!

Let's keep our Grandma's and Grandpa's as long as we can or soon these "baby-killers" will find a way to legalize the killing of our elderly too!

What's behind this God-awful killing of these little unborn babies? I'm convinced it's the love of money! Reliable sources tell me that some abortion doctors make as much as $6,000 a day, killing babies! Some abortion clinics are open around the clock! But if no doctor or nurse would be paid for these abortions, I'm persuaded this Godless killing would stop before the sun sets on another day!

These little ones belong to God. They don't belong to the mothers — even though they are giving birth to them! They sure don't belong the the doctors and nurses who are killing them or to the High Court who have legalized their murder! These Supereme Court members (and all the others involved in these killings!) shall some day soon face a Supreme God who will demand an accounting!

The deep, haunting, screams of pain from these millions of murdered little ones is so loud that I cannot hear the hollow cries of the politicians, the so-called ERA people and other misguided souls who are rushing America to God's judgment by saying, "The mother has her constitutional rights to do with her body what she pleases!"

I say, "That defenseless little unborn baby has

some rights too! That little baby has a body of it's own!''

I have no use for these liberal, left-wing politicians who try to talk out of both sides of their mouth by saying, "Personally, I'm opposed to abortion (why don't they call it what it is — killing!) but I feel the mother should have her rights to do as she pleases with her body.''

Hogwash! Would any of those politicians have wanted that kind of wicked activity taken against them before they were born? The answer is obvious!

Who then will speak up today for the little unborn baby who cannot speak up for it's self?

But you may ask, "What about the little babies who are conceived from incest and rape? Surely you favor abortion in these cases, don't you?''

Statistics reveal that less than one half of one percent of all abortions are for babies who were the result of rape or incest. You would think from the loud cries from the baby killers that almost all abortions are for these little ones!

But just suppose that today you found out you were born as a result of a "rapist" or from incest . . . would you have wanted your mother to have aborted you?

As ugly as rape and incest are, killing the baby that results will just add to this awful sin!

The tragic truth is that in most cases, abortion has become legalized murder and an alternative for birth control pills and contraceptives! This may be speaking bold, but it is high time someone started telling it like it is!

The killing of these unborn babies is bad, but what about the horrible abomination of selling these little aborted babies by the sack and by the pound out the back doors of doctor's offices, clinics and hospitals?

My concerns in this area prompted me to hire private investigators to find out what was really happening to those babies whose lives were being taken before birth.

This undercover operation was very costly, but it revealed the shocking truth that indeed, "Aborted Babies" are being sold in this country and it is a well known fact in medical circles!

My investigation uncovered the horrifying information that aborted babies are being used in research and experiments, as well as being processed into many beauty products - such as, face creams, body lotions, shampoos and hair rinse!

It's almost beyond belief! If I had not sponsored the investigation myself, I would have probably doubted it too!

This ingredient in these various products is called "collagen", "elastin", and "zyderm". What do these words mean? Webster's definition of collagen is "collagen is a fibrous protein found in connective tissue bone and cartilage." There is animal collagen, but generally if a beauty aid has animal collagen it will tell you in the small print where it lists it's contents.

Some cosmetic companies (here in the United States!) are now boldly saying on their labels their products contain "human collagen" and "human protein!" Human collagen and human protein from what? After my private investigation, I'm persuaded these ingredients are from processed aborted babies!

Recently I was told of a semi-truck driver who quit his job when he found out he was hauling aborted babies from one place to another. Though he needed the job desperately, he refused to be a part of this grisly activity!

One doctor told my investigator that, "The best collagen is from aborted babies taken alive, "C-Section" in the ninth month!" If they can be processed while they are still alive and kicking, the doctor continued, "this makes the best and most expensive collagen!"

My undercover man stated, "He said this without even blinking an eye!"

My investigation was also expanded to Europe. Here we located what is called "The world's largest fetal bank" in London. We were told that abortion clinics from around the world, quick freeze and air express their aborted babies to this "fetal bank". Here they are processed and sold as "collagen" to cosmetic companies everywhere!

Most of us, though we strongly oppose the killing of these unborn babies, now find that without even realizing it, we are aiding the killing of these babies by buying the products of those using these aborted fetuses processed into their products.

We cleaned out the shelves at our house and we have also started reading the small print on the various beauty products.

Nick Thimmeasch, syndicated columnist for the L.A. Times, recently wrote an article on this subject.

The headline read, "Human Collagen and Placenta Plus Used In Beauty Products By Cosmetic Companies!" His article tells of one well-known hospital (here in America!) which recently sold $68,000 worth of aborted babies out the back door.

I sent my camera crew to that hospital for the story. An interview with one of the nurses was progressing well until she found out this was a part of a one-hour TV special to be released nationwide. Then security was called immediately and my TV crew was ordered and physically assisted off the hospital grounds!

With God's help, I am blowing the lid on this horrifying Abortion Abomination. We must stand up and stop it or you can be sure the judgment of God will be upon us . . . swift and soon!

Yes, while America has been plalying at it's ballgames — it's cinema theaters — in front of it's TV's — in it's swimming pools — on it's beaches — at it's gambling casino's — on it's streets and highways — and yes, we have been "playing" in our churches, the thieves have been stealing our precious unborn babies, killing them and processing them into our beauty products that we smear on our faces, wash and rinse our hair with and inject into the wrinkles of our skin!

GOD HAVE MERCY!

It's time to QUIT PLAYING and start some serious praying! Holy Ghost revival is America's only hope!